INSTANT LEADS

Everything you need to know about generating more business.

By

BRADLEY J. SUGARS

Edited by
Grant McDuling

INSTANT LEADS
Copyright © 2004 by Bradley J. Sugars
Printed in Australia. No part of this book may be used or reproduced in any
manner whatsoever without prior written permission from the publisher.

ISBN 0958093210
SECOND EDITION

Published by *Action* *International* Pty Ltd
GPO Box 1340 Brisbane, QLD 4001
Phone: +61 (0) 7 3368 2525
Fax: +61 (0) 7 3368 2535
www.action-international.com

Distributed by *Action* *International* for further information
contact +61 (0) 7 3368 2525

Printed in Australia by Pure Print

Dedicated to all Action Business Coaches ...

Leaders in every sense of the word ...

■ CONTENTS

▌Introduction

One of the fundamental problems most businesses face is the generation of new leads. Without a constant supply of leads, they're faced with a never-ending battle to generate sufficient cashflow for the business to survive from one month to the next.

The average business owner spends every available minute balancing the demands of the business against those of the customers. There never seems enough time to clear the desk long enough to contemplate even the most rudimentary of plans, let alone how to grow the business.

Most business owners I talk to tell the same story: their lives resemble a see-saw with so many factors needing balancing on a daily basis. They all want the same thing; to swap this balancing act for something more predictable. And they're always stunned when I show them how easy this is to accomplish.

You see, you need to forget about all the hype you've been taught when it comes to running a business. Many of you will find this real easy, because if you're like the vast majority of business owners, you haven't been taught anything about running a business! This is a sad indictment of our education system, but, with the right attitude, it's easily fixed.

So, forget all the imagined complexities you believe running a business contains. When I analyse the countless thousands of interactions I've had with business owners over the years, there are three things, and only three, people who come to me for help, need help on. These are customers, turnover, and profit. But they are precisely the things that can't be had. These are the very things most of them spend all their days trying to influence, without success. You see, they are the most illusive of business variables.

Understand this: customers, turnover, and profit are all the result of something else in the business formula. What is the business formula? I call it the Business Chassis (read more about this in my book *Instant Cashflow*). It looks like this (refer to next page).

Notice how these illusive variables come after the equals sign in the formula. They are results; results of something else. You need to understand that if you want to change a result, you have to change what goes into it. You can't make a better cake with the same recipe. You need to change the variables – in our case the leads, the conversion rate, the number of transactions, the average dollar sale price, and the margins.

These are the only five things you need to do to grow your business.

It all starts with the number of leads you get. This book, concentrates on the first part of the Business Chassis – the leads. It shows you, in easy-to-understand steps,

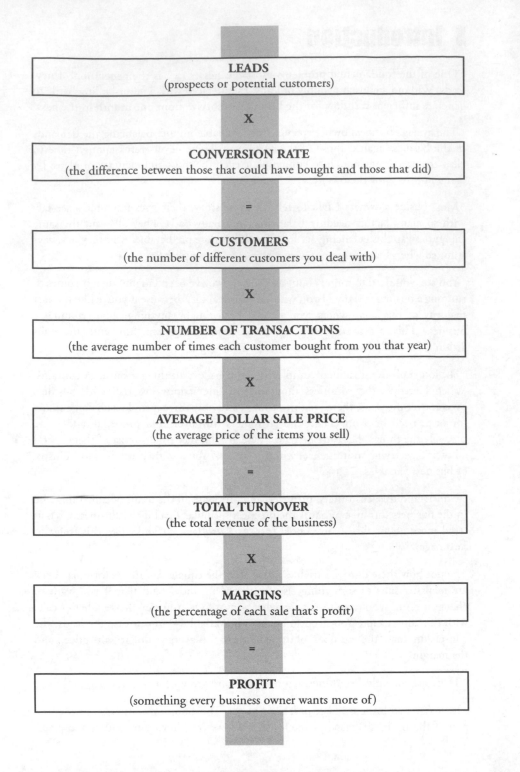

HOW to go about developing or designing great strategies that'll generate more leads for you.

It covers lead generation activities like Classifieds, Radio and Yellow Pages Advertising. It also covers lesser-known activities such as Host Beneficiaries, Strategic Alliances, Referrals, and Unique Selling Propositions and Guarantees. You'll learn all you need to know about these different lead generation activities through reading this book.

I must mention at this stage I have made a distinction between Classified Advertising and Print Advertising. They are both great lead generation tools and they are very similar in nature. The real difference between them lies in what they try to achieve. Classifieds are aiming at readers who have already decided they want to buy a particular product or service, whereas Print Advertising is aimed at people who haven't yet made that decision. Get it? Good. So for the purposes of this book, I'll be concentrating on Classified Advertising, as I believe this has got to be one of the greatest forms of advertising ever created. Why? Because through it, you get to reach millions of people at such a small cost. This means you generally have to make only one or two sales from each classified ad to make a decent profit.

The two forms of advertising are very similar from a technical point of view. Considerations you need to weigh up are very similar for both. But there are important differences. If you'd like to find out more about Print Advertising, read my book *Instant Advertising*.

Of course, there is more that can be done to find new customers. There's a wh raft of activities I categorise as PROMOTIONS. To find out more about thi my book *Instant Promotions*.

So, congratulations on deciding to take pro-active steps to develop By concentrating on first things first, you'll set in motion a chain will generate more leads for your business. I personally guarante

This book is designed to give you the inside track on ever about how to generate more leads for your business. It an INSTANT guide on how to produce the various the professionals. Once you've read the book, you'l successfully generate more leads for your busine

This book is the next step in your marketi you won't have to dream about the day field – you'll know precisely what to d how to go about ensuring your bu coming through your doors.

▌ How To Use This Book

This book is divided into different Parts, one for each of the major lead generation tools I'll be discussing.

You can work through this book from beginning to end to gain an inside track on how to find new leads for your business, just as the professionals would, or you can simply pick the one that interests you most, jump straight in and begin working through the steps outlined. Either way, you'll discover just how easy it is to get your business humming.

Each easy-to-understand step covers an important aspect of the lead generation tools being discussed. You see, there are things you must give careful consideration to before jumping in and spending money.

Of course there are certain elements that are common to all the great strategies being discussed, so these will be handled in detail in Part 10 towards the end of the book. Read them in conjunction with the various Parts of the book that deal with each relevant lead generation strategy.

You might decide to implement all the great ideas explained in this book all at once, or you might decide to implement them one at a time. But whatever you decide, the important thing is you'll no longer be blundering around in the dark, unsure whether what you're doing has a chance of bringing in more business or not.

We'll start by visiting Charlie, my trusty mechanic who was having trouble getting his head around expanding his business. Well, maybe not so much expanding it as ensuring business kept rolling in. He, like so many small business operators, was finding it frustratingly difficult balancing the demands of his business. You know – finding clients on the one hand, then servicing them on the other. This is what I call the see-saw of small business. His case is typical. See what he did to resolve these challenges.

Then read through each section of the book that deals with your chosen lead generation strategy, and jot down notes. You might also be surprised at how much this exercise will reveal about your business. It may get you thinking about important issues you've never thought about before. If some of this information is new to you, don't be concerned – there's never been a better time to start than NOW.

Make sure you make notes as you go along. When you come to designing your own lead generation strategies, you'll find it useful referring back to them. You'll find proven examples and ideas when combined with your new knowledge will bring results.

Now it's time to get started. There are customers out there waiting to deal with you. All you need is a way to convince them to do business with you.

▌ Charlie Chases Leads

It was a hot, humid morning when I pulled up outside Charlie's garage. Living in the sub-tropics has its advantages, but this certainly wasn't one of them, I decided. Thank heavens for air-conditioning.

Funny that – it struck me that I'd never previously realised just how important airconditioning was in an open sports car! Much like lead generation to a business. You see, with both you can get by without them, but life is so much more difficult. They are not obvious factors you'd think of when talking about an open sports car or a business. However, not having them means you're certain to making things harder for yourself. Use them, and you'll never look back. You'll wonder how you ever managed without them.

"G'day Charlie," I said as I applied the hand break. I let the 12-cylinder engine idle for a few moments. God, I love that sweet, burbling sound that only thoroughbred sports cars have.

Charlie loved it too. He smiled, casting an appreciative eye over my car's purposeful body before walking over and shaking me by the hand.

"Good to see you Brad. How's the car going?"

"As good as ever," I replied. "But more to the point, how's your business going?"

He had mentioned to me when I was in last having a set of new tyres fitted that he felt he was getting nowhere fast. Working his butt off seven days a week, yet not making any real progress towards attaining a better lifestyle for himself or his family. That comment resulted in a quick visit to a few local businesses that I had been working with, and Charlie seemed genuinely impressed. We visited Barry the Cake Shop Owner to see what he was doing about generating leads, Adrian the Printer to see what he was doing to increase the number of transactions his customers make, Barbara the Removalist about boosting the average dollar sale and Ryan the Sports Goods Retailer for a lesson on boosting margins.

Charlie was blown away by what he saw and decided it was time to take *Action*.

We set a date and I advised him to make sure we had uninterrupted time to really discuss what he needed to do to get his business really pumping.

He was as good as his word. His small office had been prepared for our meeting – the desk had been cleared, two chairs had been pulled up alongside each other and the coffee was on the brew.

We sat down and got straight to business.

"I'd like to begin by taking a moment to look at your lead generation strategies". I could tell by the blank look in his eyes he was beginning to feel uncomfortable already.

"What I mean by lead generation, Charlie, is the number of people who ring you up or come into your garage as a result of whatever marketing you're doing," I continued. "I don't mean those people who actually do business with you, but those who simply contact you for the first time."

"I'm with you, Brad. What would you like to know?"

"Do you test and measure the number of leads you get in a week?"

"Hell no. The only testing and measuring I do around here is back there in the workshop. As you know that's my speciality. I've got test equipment there that some of the main dealers don't have!"

Charlie was getting on a roll, but I needed to keep him on track.

"How many do you think you get on average?" I pressed on. He sank back deeper into his chair, ruffled his eyebrows and looked hard at the faded ceiling.

"Let me see now …' he whispered, sucking in deeply. "I really don't know, but it would have to be three or four."

"What advertising or marketing are you currently doing?" I continued.

"Ha, that I can tell you. See, I do know something about marketing and all that stuff. Each month I place ads in the local paper. I also do letterbox drops and occassionally I do spots on the radio."

He seemed satisfied with himself and I certainly wasn't about to burst his bubble. I wanted him to feel comfortable switching roles from mechanic to businessman even if only for a few hours each week.

"That's great, Charlie. How's that going?"

"It seems like business picks up when we run the advertising and I get in all these cars to tune. But by the time I've worked my way through them, there's a trough at the end of the month – you know, not enough business to keep my four mechanics busy. I have to hope like mad a few jobs turn up just to pay the overheads."

A very common problem I thought, but fortunately one that's easily taken care of.

"What have you done in the past that hasn't worked?"

"Plenty, Brad. Mostly things like local sponsorships, a bit of cinema advertising and I also had a whole batch of fridge magnets made."

"Why do you think they didn't work?"

"Dunno, Brad. That's why I've got you here."

"Let me put it another way then. Do you know for sure they didn't work?"

"Of course they didn't. They were a big waste of money, I can tell you. I'll never try them again."

I could see he wasn't really sure. He was beginning to feel uncomfortable again and began shifting around in his chair. It was time for me to talk generally about lead generation and the part it plays in business.

"You've actually been doing quite well, Charlie. So far you've been really close to the mark. But you just haven't gone far enough. So don't worry, you haven't wasted any money at all. In fact, my view is that you've been making good marketing investments that we can work with, add to and develop to their full potential." His eyes were alight and his shoulders pulled back.

"Let me explain why. As you already know, the term 'leads' refers to the total number of potential buyers you contacted, or who contacted you. Some people refer to them as prospects or potential customers. We're talking about the same group of people here. In your case, these are the people who receive your advertising material or heard your radio ads and did something as a result. They might have phoned up to enquire further or they might have given consideration to having their car serviced here.

"Most businesses confuse responses with results. You see, just because the ads have caused your phone to ring, doesn't mean your cash register will. But what really amazes me is how few businesses actually know how many leads they get each week. How about you, Charlie?"

"I know exactly what you're saying, Brad. You're spot on. After my ads run, the phone sure runs hot. And I get business – but just how many phone in yet don't make a booking, I'm not quite sure. I've never thought to make a note of that."

"Here's your first lesson, Charlie. Always take down each caller's contact details. If you do this, you'll be well on your way to developing your own database of prospects that will result into a big money-spinner for you. You see, all these people have an interest in what you do, otherwise they wouldn't have bothered to respond. Would they? The fact they didn't go further and book their cars in doesn't matter. They might not have been in a position to do so just then. They might still have been shopping around for the best garage, by not following them up, your sending them a message that you don't really care about having them as a customer."

"But Brad, I just don't have the time and I'll bet none of my competitors do either."

"That's precisely it, Charlie. Don't you see that one of the great ways to win business is to be different from the pack? You have to establish and promote a unique selling proposition, or USP as it's known. By going the extra mile and doing things slightly differently to other garages, you'll not only stand out, you'll also give the impression you actually care about your prospects. You'll also greatly increase your chances of them coming to you when they're ready."

Charlie was beginning to catch on.

"Developing a list of leads is one thing, doing something with them is another. But that's jumping ahead a little. What we're talking about right now is how to go about gathering a useful number of leads from which you can work. What we're focusing on is how to go about getting people to make contact with you in the first place. Are you with me, Charlie?"

"I'm right there, Brad. Keep talking, mate."

"I have a proven list of over 70 ways of generating leads for any business. They range from newspaper advertising to public relations campaigns, from direct mail drops to participating at market days. But obviously, some will be more applicable to your business than others. And it also would make better business sense if we were to focus our efforts on a few to begin with. Isn't that right, Charlie?"

"If you say so, Brad. Keep talking."

"What we're going to do now Charlie is to talk about a number of strategies I believe you should think about implementing into your business. They're all really easy to understand and put into place. They really do work. We're going to talk about classified advertising, running a radio campaign, advertising in the Yellow Pages, setting up a host beneficiary strategy, establishing a strategic alliance, putting in place a referral strategy, developing a USP and guarantee. I'm also going to show you how to write killer headlines and create powerful offers. Once we've been through all this, I'll show you how to do a Break Even Analysis to ensure the costs are in line with the benefits received."

"That sounds like a heck of a lot, mate. I don't know if all this is up my street. I'm only a mechanic."

"Don't worry, Charlie. You'll get to grips with this real easily. But more importantly, when you start to see the benefits it'll have on your business, you'll be blown away. That I promise."

"OK, Brad. Let's get into it then."

Part 1

▌ Classified Advertising

"Charlie, I'm going to start with Classified Advertising, if that's OK?"

"Fine by me, Brad. At least it's something I know a bit about, having done a fair bit of it over the years."

That was exactly my reasoning, and it was working.

"I thought we'd start with the familiar and then progress to the not-so-familiar, if you follow my drift."

"I'm right there with you, mate. You lead the way."

My strategy is always to go right back to basics. That way there's little chance of anything falling through the cracks.

"I'm going to start by looking at what Classified Advertising really is, and what makes it successful. Then we'll consider exactly what you need to do to ensure yours is a success. How does that sound?"

"Beautiful mate. Let's get into it."

What Is A Successful Classified Advertisement?

Classified advertising is one of the most cost effective lead generation tools any business can use. It commands greater confidence than almost any other form of advertising. The true beauty of the classified section in most newspapers is that people who are reading them are doing so, because they want to buy a particular product or service.

Unlike normal print advertising where you're trying to convince people they need what you're selling. People reading the classifieds have already made the decision to buy.

They're qualified customers looking for a deal. All you have to do is get them to deal with you.

So what makes a successful classified advertisement?

Basically any classified advertisement that pays for itself can be considered successful. That's not to say our objective is to spend $100 and get $100 worth of sales as a result of it. What you need to understand is the lifetime value of each customer who responds to your ad.

Think of it this way: You acquire customers through classified ads. Your acquisition cost is determined by how much your classified advertisement costs, divided by how many customers it brings into your store.

Once you've calculated this figure, you can work out how many times each customer needs to purchase from you before they become profitable. In the average business this will mean selling to them 2 times before you begin to make a profit.

With this in mind, you need to focus on bringing the customer back on a regular basis. Therefore, any classified advertisement that covers its cost initially will turn out to be profitable in the long-term.

What Makes A Successful Classified Ad?

There are a number of key elements which, when combined, make a successful classified advertisement. The most important of these is the headline. You'll find out everything you need to know about how to write effective headlines in Part 8.

Another important consideration is the offer you're making. No matter how well written your classified advertisement is, without a great offer it will not work.

In the following pages you'll learn how to write headlines that work, how to position your advertisement for maximum exposure and which typefaces have the best recognition levels. You'll also discover which category your classified advertisement should appear in, what size to use and which benefits, angles and appeals work best.

The 7 Steps To Classified Advertising Success

Step 1: Who (Is Your Target Market)?

Before you begin designing your classified ad, you need to have a clear idea of whom it is you are trying to reach? You need to know exactly who your target market is. If you don't, it's almost impossible to attract them. You'd have to take the 'let's see' approach. Unfortunately, the 'let's see' method of advertising tends to fail every time. One thing is certain; you won't see anything in the way of new customers.

You need to know exactly who you're dealing with, what they're interested in and what's going to make them buy your product. If you don't know these basic facts, you're really just taking your chances.

So let's get specific. Who are the people most likely to be interested in your product or service? Here are some guidelines.

Age: How old are they? Don't just say 'all ages' or 'a variety'. We want to create a picture in mind of your average customer. Think of an age that symbolises most of your customers.

Sex: Are they male or female? 'Half and half' is too broad. Practically every business is split one way or the other. Give it some real thought. Which gender spends more with you and visits more often?

Income: How much do they make? Do they earn a great living, meaning quality is the big issue, or are they scraping for every dollar, always looking for a deal? It's essential you find this out.

Where do they live: Are they local, or do they come from miles around to deal with you? This will dictate how you communicate with them.

Step 2: Where (To Run Your Classified Advertisement)?

Now you've identified the 'who' you need to find a publication that reaches them. There may be a number of seemingly suitable publications. To find out which works best for you, try them all and then test and measure the results. You'll find out all you need to know about testing and measuring in Part 10.

Newspapers are among the most common classified advertising mediums for the small to medium sized business, although some trade publications may also have a section for classifieds. Newspaper advertising can be relatively expensive, particularly in metropolitan markets. Basically, there are two types of newspapers for you to choose from although there may only be one in some regional centres.

Daily Newspapers

The first of these are daily newspapers. These are papers that are printed six or seven days a week, but be aware that circulation can vary greatly from day to day. For example, a paper's circulation (number of papers sold each day) may be 45,000 on a Saturday and only 23,500 on a Monday.

Classified Advertising

Weekly Newspapers

The second type is weekly newspapers. These are only printed once a week and are quite often delivered free of charge to homes. Because weekly newspapers are delivered to specific areas, they can be a great advertising tool for tradesmen, accountants, hairdressers, and other similar types of businesses.

Daily newspapers tend to have a larger circulation, because their articles are more up to date. They will also tend to attract a readership within a wealthier demographic than weekly papers would. If you're selling more expensive items, luxury services or have a sale that only lasts a few days, then daily newspapers are definitely more effective than weekly publications. If on the other hand you're selling less expensive items or clearing out old stock, weekly papers can bring a good response.

It's also worth keeping in mind that many people actually refer to their weekly paper when looking for certain services rather than consulting the Yellow Pages. This is because it's easier to find tradesmen or service people in a specific suburb from the local paper, than it is by wading through all the entries listed in the Yellow Pages.

Magazines

Because most magazines are national publications, they will generally be very expensive and the majority of them won't have a classified section. The major benefit of classified advertising in magazines is that they target people with specific interests. Magazines are great if you sell your product nationally, have a high price or a target-specific product or service.

For example, a company that manufactures bullbars could advertise in the classified section of a 4WD magazine, or a hose manufacturer could advertise in the classified section of a gardening magazine. Magazine advertising can also be very effective for companies that sell by mail order.

Trade Journals

Trade journals are one of the least expensive forms of classified advertising. Companies advertising in them have the advantage of being able to reach a very specific target market. Whilst this is a benefit, it can also be a limitation as they generally won't have a very high readership. To use trade journals effectively, you need to have a great offer. But, keep in mind not all trade journals have a classified section.

In addition to the large number of publications you have to choose from, you'll also have a number of classifications to decide between. As an example, a typical daily newspaper has the following classified sections:

Accessories for Motor Vehicles

Amusements

Announcements

Auctions

Births

Business Opportunities

Church Notices

Commercial and Industrial Properties

Commission Only Vacancies

Domestic Work Wanted

Engagements

Fathers Day Greetings

For Hire

Florists

For Rent

Garage Sale

Getting Married

Horses and Gear

Holiday Resorts

In Memoriam

Licensed Tradesmen Available

Marine

Motorcycles

Motor Vehicle Maintenance

Mothers Day Greetings

Pets and Supplies

Photographers

Professional Notices

Positions Vacant

Real Estate

Stock

Sub-Contracting

Tradesmen

Twenty-First Birthdays

Thank You Notices

Wanted To Buy

Wedding

Accommodation

Anniversaries

Antiques

Birthdays

Business For Sale

Caravans and Trailers

Christmas Greetings

Computers Congratulations

Deaths

Employment Services

Funeral Directors

Finance

Farm Goods and Services

Funerals

For Sale

Garden Supplies

Hire Cars

Home Improvements

Home and Office Supplies

Lost and Found

Legal Notices

Memorial Services

Motor Vehicles

Music

Open Weekends

Personal

Poultry

Public Notices

Positions Wanted

Sport and Gear

St.Valentine's Day

Vacancies

Training and Tuition

Trucks and Machinery

Tenders

Wanted To Rent

Work Wanted

Classified Advertising

These are just some of the many categories you may have to choose from. You need to make sure you place your ad in the section where people will be looking for that product or service. If no suitable category exists, place you advertisement in another section that might be read by your target market.

Step 3: What (Do You Want To Say)?

This may ruffle a few feathers. There's no such thing as 'image advertising.' Be aware it's just a concept newspapers and marketing people have invented to explain advertising that doesn't do a thing for your business or make you a cent. It's the ad that says: 'Hi, our name is this, we sell this type of product, our phone number is this,' and it's a total waste of time.

You need to say something to your potential customers. There must be a strong message you're trying to get across to people. This may be in the form of a strong offer you want to make, an important point of difference, a list of the benefits that result when dealing with you, or something unusual about your product.

It's essential WHAT you say is appealing to WHO you are trying to say it to. For example, giving away a skateboard with each walking frame sold probably won't work. Giving away an arthritis ointment however, would probably get great results.

Let's deal with each type of message, one by one.

Strong Offer: This is the most commonly used and the one that tends to work the best. Remember people are generally looking for the product or service that offers the best value for money. So an ad with an offer that stops them in their tracks can get outstanding results. You'll learn more about creating powerful offers in Part 10.

Point Of Difference: This can work well when there is a large market for your product and where you have many competitors. For example, if you were advertising a 'steak and seafood' restaurant, you'd be hard pressed to stand out. But what if your steakhouse had live entertainment, free drinks from 7pm and the best view in town? That would be worth promoting.

Listing The Benefits: If you don't have a strong offer or point of difference, listing the benefits of dealing with you may do the trick. For example, a plumber could list the four ways he gives better service, or a beauty salon could emphasise the six ways a client's skin will improve after only one visit. Most importantly, you must relate the benefits to the customer. Remember; always write your classified ad about the reader's favourite subject - THEM.

People will normally read the headline first, the sub-headlines next and finally the coupon or PS. You can often get people to go back and read the copy by making a strong, clear offer in your coupon.

Borders

Most newspapers will have a wide variety of borders from which to choose. Whilst an unusual border can help your ad standout, one that is too elaborate can get in the way of your selling message.

A particularly successful classified border is simply a dotted line around the ad. The reason it works so well is that people are used to cutting around dotted lines. By using a dotted line border you're ensuring there's a greater chance the ad will get cut out and used later.

Pictures

Studies have shown that ads containing a picture that takes up between 25% and 75% of the total area of the advertisement have greater readerships than those without one. You will need to put a fair amount of text in your ad, so 25% is probably the ideal size. Don't use line drawings or clipart. Photographs get a much higher response rate than illustrations.

Consider putting a photograph of yourself in the ad. People buy from people, not companies, so let them see the person behind the company name. Place your photograph so it looks straight out of the page or towards your body copy. If your picture is looking into your ad, your potential customers will also be drawn into it. And always put a caption under your photograph. Everybody reads the captions; so make sure you take advantage of this opportunity to get them into your ad. Once again this only applies to display classified advertisements.

If you're using a photograph of a similar make or model to the product you're selling, but not a photograph of the actual product itself, you need to state this clearly at the bottom of your ad. You must place an asterisk (*) underneath or alongside the photograph. Most advertisers then say in a caption at the bottom of their ad: '* Pictures for comparison purposes only.' This is particularly important when advertising motor vehicles. For example, if you run a photograph of a 1994 Ford Falcon with a roof rack and the actual car you're selling doesn't have a roof rack, important you indicate the picture is for comparison purposes only.

ing Out What Works

n you've finished your ad, it's time to test and measure. Start off testing both adline and your offer by running small ads and measuring the response. Test nse you get to each headline and each offer, then combine the best ones and classified ad at full size.

Step 4: How (To Write Your Classified Advertisement)

Now that you've covered the basics, it's time to get into the nuts and bolts of how to write your classified advertisement.

There are three basic types of classified advertisements:

1. Display classified advertisements are very similar to standard print advertisements.

2. Semi-display advertisements are basically line ads with a border around them.

3. Line ads are commonly used for private sales.

Headline

The most important part of your advertisement is the headline. David Ogilvy, one of the all time great direct response copywriters, once said that 10 times as many people would read the headline as will read the rest of the ad. So if you get the headline wrong, you can kiss 90% of your advertising dollars goodbye.

You will find out more about writing headlines in Part 10. However, at this point you need to keep in mind when running a display classified advertisement, is that the headline needs to take up at least 25% of the total size of your advertisement. If however, you're running a simple line ad, your headline or first word should immediately tell the reader what it is you're trying to sell.

Typefaces

The typeface (or font as it is otherwise known) you use in your advertisement can make a big difference to the results you achieve. Typefaces can basically fall into one of two categories: Sans Serif and Serif. Sans Serif fonts don't have the little "feet" at the bottom of each letter.

Studies have shown that people find sans serif fonts far more difficult to read than serif fonts, because serif fonts have the little "feet" or "hooks" at the bottom of each letter. These appear to form a line under the words that your eye can follow as you read. If you want people to read your classified advertisement, use a serif typeface.

The most common serif font is Times New Roman. Find out the font used by the publication your ad's running in and have your ad set in that font.

Point Size

The size of the font you use is referred to as its point size. Studies have shown readership does not drop off between 14 and 7? point size. As a general rule, I'd recommend you use 10 point fonts. However, if you're running a line ad, you may wish to use an impact headline that would be a much larger point size. You'll learn more about this shortly.

Highlighting Text

Use bold type to highlight key points in your copy, headlines and sub-headlines. Italics can also be used to highlight key areas of text, although it can be hard to read and should only be used sparingly. Never use ALL CAPITALS (sometimes referred to as Upper Case.)

The only time you can use all capitals is in a short or impact headline, or for the extra emphasis of a key word.

If you're running a display advertisement, you may wish to break your copy up into paragraphs, as this will make it easier to read. Indenting your paragraphs rather than leaving a line between them, can cut down on wasted space. Also consider using a drop cap first letter, as it's a great way to attract the eye of your reader.

Sub-Headlines

Sub-headlines have three major benefits:

1. They break up large blocks of text, making them easier to read. If your display classified advertisement looks like one big 'chunk' of text it can put people off reading it. By using sub-headlines, you can break your copy up and give it some 'space.'

2. They allow someone skimming over your classified ad to only read the points that interest them.

3. They spark the reader's interest. If your headline doesn't get them in completely, you can get a second chance with your sub-headlines.

It is important your sub-headlines tell a story. They need to be able to convey your message to those people who are just browsing over your ad. Obviously you would only use sub-headlines in display classified advertisements, as line ads are normally not long enough to warrant them.

Body Copy

You only get one chance with a potential customer, so your first few words are crucial. You must get your reader interested immediately with the very first paragraph. If they're not excited after the first 50 words or so, they won't read the rest of your ad.

Use the bare minimum of words to get your message across. Don't waffle on. But make sure you include enough information to get your reader interested enough to call you. Never tell the whole story in your ad. Tell them only as much as you need to, in order to get them to call. By holding back some information, you make it necessary for them to call to find out more.

Your ad should tell your prospects exactly what it is that you're trying to sell them. When you finish writing your ad, get someone to look over it and critique it for you. Only make one offer in your ad, but make it exciting!

Abbreviations

Using abbreviations in line and semi-display classified ads is an effective way to cut down on your costs. You also must be careful not to abbreviate words to the extent that the reader becomes confused. Only use abbreviations that are commonly understood. These are ones people are generally familiar with. Here are some examples:

access - accessories	excel cond - excellent condition
vgc - very good condition	rrp - recommended retail price
BH - business hours	AH - after hours
alum - aluminium	4WD - four wheel drive
good cond - good condition	p-steer - power steering
ac - air conditioning	cc - cruise control
kms - kilometres	auto - automatic
SWB - short wheelbase	LWB - long wheelbase
2-m-o - two months old	1-y-o - one year old
t-bred - thoroughbred	ono - or nearest offer
obo - or best offer	hh - hands high
reg - registered	Lic No - license number

You may not be allowed to abbreviate some words by law. If you're un should check with your local newspaper.

Coupons

Coupons are a great way to measure the success of your ca getting coupons back, your classified ad's not working. Bec only briefly look over your display classified ad, you n in the coupon.

Most companies get tired of their ad before the consumer does. As long as your ad's working, don't change it. There is a constant turnover of readers for each publication, so stick to a successful formula for as long as you can.

To get an idea of ads that are working, look for the ones that run day after day, week after week. If an ad's been running for a long time, chances are it's working.

Step 5: How Big (Should Your Classified Ad Be)?

There's a lot more to working out the size than most people think. Usually, it's a case of: 'How much can we afford?'

The question really should be: 'How much do we want to make?' If the ad is good enough, it should make you money not drain your funds.

Basically, when you're looking to run a classified advertisement you have the choice between doing line ads, semi-display ads or display classified ads. Semi-display ads are basically just line ads with a border. So let's look at the best size for each:

Display Classified Advertisements

If you don't have an ad you know works, you need to guess. You need to think about how many responses you need to 'break-even.' This means how many sales do you need to pay back the advertising cost?

Here's how you work it out. Firstly, you need to work out your average profit. To do this, measure the amount of profit on each sale, every day for three days. Then, find the average. If you want to skip the hard work estimate this figure.

Next, choose a standard ad size. If it's for a newspaper, find out the price on a 15 x 2 (15cm deep and 2 columns wide). If you're dealing with a magazine, get the price on a quarter page ad.

Now, divide the ad cost by your average profit. This will give you the number of sales you need to pay for the ad.

Here's an example. Let's say a hairdresser makes about $15 profit from each haircut. They take out an ad that costs $270. That means they need 18 new customers from the ad. Anything less and the ad is losing them money.

Of course, it's not a hard and fast rule you must break even on every ad. In the case of the hairdresser, they'd probably be happy with nine new loyal customers. After each has been in twice, they'd probably become profitable.

This is called lifetime value. It's the amount a customer spends with you over the course of their lifetime. In the case of a business with a high level of repeat business like hairdressers, restaurants, or mechanics, it might be worth losing money the first time, just to gain a new customer. This customer may ultimately be worth thousands.

If you get out of 'break-even' thinking and into 'lifetime value' mode, a whole new world of possibilities open up. If you're confident you'll get these new customers back again, you can afford to offer something incredible and make a dead loss the first time they come in. Once you've established whether you have to break-even or whether you can afford to rely on the lifetime value of the customer, you are then in a position to make a decision about size.

Let's look at a break-even situation first.

To decide how big your classified ad should be, you have to guess how many replies you're likely to get. This can be tricky, especially if you haven't had a lot of experience with advertising before. In fact, even if you've advertised many times before, it can still be tricky. You can only really rely on what you've done before, the responses your competitors seem to get, and your instinct.

In the end, it all comes down to probability. Let's say you sell pizzas with a profit margin of $1.20. Taking out an ad that costs $120 means you need 100 new customers to pay for it. You need to judge whether that's likely to happen. If you ran an ad last year and got only five replies, it's looking pretty improbable.

In some cases, you may realise that breaking even is near impossible. In this case, you have to either think about lifetime value or advertising somewhere else.

The other thing to consider is this: newspapers and magazines with high advertising rates usually have high readership levels. It's not as if you're paying more for nothing. If you were to go with a cheaper paper, you're likely to get a lower response rate.Once you've weighed all this up, consider how much space you actually need. How much text is in your ad? How big are the other ads on the page? Will you be seen if you go small? Do your pictures need to be a certain size?

If you need more space than you can reasonably afford, you may need to look at a different approach. By this I mean another creative approach. Perhaps you could take the picture out and trim some of the text.

Lastly, it's important to start small and work your way up. Design your ad large enough so it has a good chance of working, but not so large that you'll go bankrupt if it bombs. Take all this into account and decide upon a size for your first ad.

Semi-Display And Line Ads

The same principle of lifetime value vs. the cost of the advertisement applies to these ads as it does to display classified ads. The main consideration with these is the minimum number of words you need to get your message across.

Line ads are normally charged at $(x) / per line. For example, if your advertisement was seven lines long and the line rate of that paper was $4.65 per line, the total cost of your advertisement would be $32.55. The number of words you can fit on any one line varies from paper to paper. Obviously the length of the words you choose will also make a difference.

To give you an example of how this works, let's look at a publication with a column width of 38cm. Using their average point size, you'll get 25 characters to one line. A character counts as anything from a letter to a full stop or space.

So let's look at running an ad that says: 'Television set, 51cm, colour complete with stand, $150 o.n.o. Phone Tim on (00) 0000 0000.'

This advertisement has 90 characters in it. Understanding we can fit 25 characters to a line, this ad would therefore take up 3.6 lines. You can't have .6 of a line, so it's rounded off to 4 lines. If the line rate for that particular newspaper were $4.65 per line, this advertisement would cost you a total of $18.60.

It's worth noting that using bold in the first one or two words will not normally cost any extra.

Line ads and semi-display ads are an inexpensive form of advertising. They can also be a great way for you to test a publication before you start to run a full-size, display classified advertisement.

Step 6: When (To Run Your Ad)

If your product is perennial (that is, it's not seasonal), you don't have to be too concerned about when you run your ad. It's more a question of which day, rather than which time of year.

You'll probably pay different rates for different days. You need to take into consideration the circulation of the different papers, and how many more readers you're getting for your money.

Also, major newspapers usually have different lift-out sections each day of the week, some of which may have a classified section. You may want to place your ad in one of these special sections. This can yield good results, although many of your competitors might be right next to you.

If your business is seasonal, you need to approach advertising differently. For example, a swimming pool builder would find it fruitless running a 'summer ad' in winter. The business owner would need to adapt the appeal to suit the time of year.

You also need to consider any major events that may be coming up. For instance, advertising sports merchandise the day before the grand final would work well. The number of times you run your advertisement in a week also needs to be considered, especially if you're advertising in a daily paper. Some days will normally have higher circulation rates than others, but repetition can also be useful. For example, a plumber who only advertises on a Wednesday may miss out on some business if three people had plumbing problems on the Monday.

Most daily newspapers will offer special rates for customers who run the same advertisement a number of times in the same week. For example, if you ran an ad that cost $20.00 for one day, it may only cost you an extra $13.40 to run it the next day as well. You may have to book in all your ads in advance to get the special rate rather than booking them in one day at a time.

Step 7: What Else (Do You Need To Think About)?

Use this section as a final checklist. Once you're happy with your classified ad, run through and make sure you're ready to get started. Here are a few things you may not have thought of:

Production: For example, you may need to take some new photographs. Don't compromise here. People interpret a lot from photographs and a bad one can really put them off. If the publication wants finished artwork, you may need to send them a 'bromide.' This is a 'flat or dull' copy of the ad printed on special paper. Phone a printer and ask for some advice here. Also, make sure you check everything before it goes to print. Ask for a 'proof' (finished copy) from the publication and check it thoroughly. Don't let anything go out with spelling mistakes or the wrong phone number (you'll be amazed how many times this happens.) Having said that, you probably won't be able to get a proof of a line or semi-display ad.

Phone Scripts: There are hundreds of cases where a classified ad made the phone ring off the hook, but the business owner saw very few sales at the end of the day. It's all to do with 'conversion'. That is, how many inquiries you turn into sales. You need a script. This is a printed version of what you say to encourage people to buy. Just think about the best sales lines you've ever used and compile them into one typed script. Make sure you ask lots of 'open-ended' questions. These are ones that start with who, what, where, when or why. Give a copy to every member of your team and make sure they USE it. It is also imperative you make sure your team know that an advertisement has been placed. This way they'll EXPECT calls.

Check Stock And Team Levels: It's unlikely your classified ad will bring in hundreds of people (very few actually do), but you do need to be prepared for a sizable response. There would be nothing worse than running a successful ad, then running out of stock or being too busy to service these new inquiries. Plan for the ad in advance. Make sure you cater for any increased demand.

Legal Requirements: One thing you need to be mindful of when advertising in the classified section of a newspaper, is your legal obligations. The laws surrounding classified advertising are quite strict. For example, car dealers who advertise in the Motor Vehicle section of the classifieds are required by law to state their business name, license number and address or phone number. Licensed clubs must have the words "For the information of members and their guests," in their classified ads. If you're uncertain about the wording of your advertisement, or your legal obligations, ask your local newspaper.

"So Charlie, has that made you feel more confident about designing a winning Classified Ad?"

"Hell yes, mate. It actually seems like common sense, now that you've explained it properly to me. I know exactly what I'm going to say in my next Classified Ad. Mind if I take a few minutes now to knock it into shape?"

"Go for it, mate. That's what this is all about."

I could tell Charlie was actually beginning to enjoy himself. He seemed to have forgotten all about his workshop and had succeeded in extracting himself away from the job. So far so good. A quick glance through the office window and I could tell his mechanics were getting on with running the show. They seemed to be enjoying having to shoulder the extra responsibility, too.

Charlie was having fun. His pencil worked furiously and in no time at all he was done.

"Great work, Charlie! I can see you're grasping the principles real quick. I reckon that ad's ready to be submitted to the local paper right now."

Here's Charlie's First Classified Advertisement:

Attention Car Owners

Here's 4 reasons why you should join Charlie's Garage's VIP Club ...

If you're tired of poor quality workmanship and inflated prices, you need to see Charlie's Garage. Here are just 4 of the many benefits you'll receive ...

1. **Free car wash & vacuum with each service.**
2. **Every 4th service free.**
3. **Two free wheel alignments each year.**
4. **Sensational monthly specials.**

So don't put up with poor service any longer. Come in and see us today at Shop 7, 77 Smith Rd, Smithsville. Or call us on:

Phone: 1234 5678

Double Column Semi-Display Classified Advertisement.

Examples

Here are a few examples of Classified advertisements designed with one thing in mind – making you money.

Study them carefully, keeping in mind what you've just discovered about writing Classified ads. You'll notice how they focus on listing the key benefits to each product or service.

You'll also notice each has a headline that delivers a selling message rather than listing the company name at the top. Look over these ads and refer back to them when writing your own.

Place Your Headline Here

Lorem et iusto odio dignissim qui blandit praesent luptatum zzril delenit au gue duis dolore te feugat nulla facilisi. Ut wisi enim ad orpersuscipit lobortis nisl ut aliqu ip ex en commodo consequat. Duis te feugifacilisi.per

Address Here
Phone Fax

Headline Goes Here

Place your Here's Why or 4 reasons sub-headline here

Lorem et iusto odio dignissim qui blandit praesent luptatum zzril delenit au gue duis dolore te feugat nulla facilisi. Ut wisi enim ad orpersuscipit lobortis nisl ut aliqu ip ex en commodo consequat.

Duis te feugifacilisi.per. yj tyjk tyjkt rth yjetyjt. Jhb rg sfgn lobortis nisl ut aliqu ip ex en commodo dfg db consequat. Duis te feugifacilisi.per. yj tyjk dghmdgm. The eh tyj fsbn yj tyuk gfjmyu.

Phone Number

$$\boxed{\textbf{Part 2}}$$

▌Radio Campaign

"OK Charlie, now we're going to look ad running a radio campaign. We're going to work through everything you need to know to writing radio commercials that will not only generate a response, but also make you money. How does that sound mate?"

"Fantastic, Brad. If it's as easy as writing a Classified Ad, then what are we waiting for?"

"As you'll discover, Charlie, it's dead simple. You'll find you'll have a whole lot of fun writing them. You see, you get to play with things like sound effects, music and other mood-creating techniques as well."

"I should have been doing this years ago, Brad. I've been missing out on the best part of business."

"You could have been doing a lot better, financially. But don't cry over spilt milk. There's never been a better time to start than right now."

What Is A Successful Radio Campaign?

Many business owners believe radio should be used to build brand or company awareness. This is a myth created by radio sales people to encourage the unsuspecting customer to spend more money. It's also a good way to avoid being held accountable for the success or otherwise of your campaign.

But not all radio stations run their business this way. Some actually sell on the basis of measurable results. These are the stations to look for.

Basically, any radio campaign that pays for itself can be considered successful. But before embarking on any radio campaign there are a few things you need to understand.

Work Out Your Costs

There are two basic costs you'll incur when advertising on radio. Obviously, you have to pay for the time your commercials are actually on air (airtime). You'll also need to pay to have the commercials produced (production costs).

Prices vary between metropolitan and regional stations, but as a general rule of thumb, you can expect to pay between $50 and $100 to have your commercials produced by the station. However, having them produced by an advertising agency can cost substantially more. Whilst you can make substantial savings by dealing directly with the station, it's important to remember an expensive commercial that works is better than a cheap one that gets little or no response.

Unlike other forms of advertising, you need to spend a minimum amount before you begin to see any worthwhile results. You can expect to spend approximately $2000 per week in a regional market and around $3000 a week with a metropolitan station. To spend any less is a waste of money. You simply won't get the repetition required to achieve a result. Repetition is important in radio advertising, so you need to make sure your commercials are played on a regular basis. You also need to look at factors like the extra team members you may need when doing specific promotions.

Know Your Margins

You need to know the net profit you make from anyone who buys your product or service. By understanding how much you actually make from each sale, you'll be able to work out how many new customers you need to make your campaign profitable.

Life Time Value

Don't view each new customer that your campaign brings in as a once-off sale. You'll normally lose money on the first sale to a new client. Remember, the average business will need to sell to a client 2 times before it begins to make a profit from them.

With this in mind, you need to focus on bringing the customer back on a regular basis. Therefore, any radio campaign that covers its cost initially will turn out to be profitable in the long-term. You'll find out how to do this in the Break Even Calculation covered in Part 10.

What Makes A Successful Radio Campaign?

Understanding that our aim is to at least cover the cost of your campaign, we need to look at the individual components that make up the campaign. We'll deal with them one by one in a moment, but first we need to identify them individually.

Targeted Demographic

You don't want to advertise on a station where the listening audience is of an age or sex that would not be interested in your product or service.

Sound Effects

This is an important part of your radio commercial. If it doesn't grab your reader's interest immediately, your campaign will probably fail.

Copy

Once your sound effects have attracted the attention of your listener, you need to convey the benefits of buying your product or services in a clear, believable and easy-to-understand fashion.

Music

Your music should appeal to the target you're aiming at. It should also compliment the product or service you're trying to sell. For example, a funeral home wouldn't use dance music.

In the pages that follow, you'll learn how to find which station has a higher market share of the listeners you're interested in reaching. You will be shown, in easy-to-follow steps, how to write effective commercials, how to structure your copy for maximum impact and the type of sound effects and music you should use in your commercial.

Then by referring to Part 10, you'll discover the types of offers that'll get the phone running hot and those that don't. I'll also give you practical tips on how to deal with radio stations. And lastly, I'll provide you with a number of templates for you to use to create your own successful radio campaign.

The 7 Steps To Writing Great Radio Commercials

Step 1: Why (Use Radio)?

Before doing anything, you need to work out whether radio is for you.

You need to compare the potential returns you expect from it against other those of other available lead generation strategies. For example; if your market is small and your offer appeals to only a select group of people, why not use direct mail instead? It's easier and probably cheaper too. Or what about a host beneficiary strategy?

Radio is ideal when you wish to reach a broad market. For example; a hardware store that sells everything from power tools to crockery would benefit from radio's ability to reach the mass market. Basically, any company that has a product or service that appeals to the mass market can benefit from using radio.

Radio Campaign

On the other hand, radio is probably inappropriate for a management consultant as the target market is so small. Direct Mail would be more appropriate.

Whilst radio is a stand alone medium in its own right, it is often beneficial to back up radio campaigns with a print campaign. This is not a hard and fast rule, however. Your promotion can be very effective using radio alone. But if it's complete coverage you're after, radio backed up with some advertisements in your local paper can produce excellent results.

So now we understand why we're using radio, let's have a look at exactly who we're after.

Step 2: Who (Is Your Target Market)?

Before you look at investing money in an advertising campaign, you need to identify exactly whom it is you're trying to reach. Precisely, who is your target market?

A failure to answer this question will cost you hundreds in wasted dollars and lead to a poor conversion rate. For example, imagine a company that sells electric wheel chairs advertising on a radio station that has a listening audience between the ages of 20 and 35. To avoid costly mistakes, you need to know who your potential customers are before you even speak to a radio salesperson.

Knowing your target market will also enable you to choose the station that reaches more of your potential clients. It also helps you write your commercial in a way your prospects will relate to. Using terms and phrases that are commonly used by your prospects will greatly increase the effectiveness of your campaign.

So let's get specific. Who are the people most likely to be interested in your product or service? Here are some guidelines:

Age: How old are they?

Sex: Are they male or female?

Income: How much do they make?

Where do they live: Are they local, or do they come from miles around to deal with you?

Step 3: Where (Do You Find A Suitable Radio Station)?

Now you've identified the 'who,' you need to find a way of reaching them. Although there are probably many stations from which to choose, not all will suit your needs.

There is basically only one thing to consider when choosing a station. Which one reaches more of your potential customers?

This is a point often forgotten when people decide to advertise on radio. Don't advertise on a particular station just because you like the music. If you're 25 years old and your customers are generally over the age of 40, chances are the station which plays the music you like won't attract any listeners in your customers demographic.

To find out which stations attract more of your target market, you need to ask each station two questions:

1. Which demographic is your programming aimed at? Every radio station has a clearly defined demographic that their programming is aimed at. What you need to understand is that whilst a station may have a target demographic of females aged 20 - 35; their programming will also appeal to other demographics with similar tastes in music. For example, a station with a demographic such as the one I've just mentioned may also attract males of a similar age group as well as people aged outside this range.

   It's probably worthwhile explaining what we mean by programming. Basically this is a combination of the type of music they play, the regular 'spots' they have each day (such as a breakfast show, mid-mornings, etc) and the types of competitions they run. In total, it means the overall sound of the station.

2. Ask to see their most recent survey figures. These figures need to have been gathered by an independent research company, such as AGB McNair. Most radio stations will interpret these figures in a way that best suits their needs. To ensure the information you're receiving is accurate, you need to see the figures for yourself and ask to have them explained to you. From there, you can make your own decision.

Of course, another useful way to decide is to simply ask your existing customers. You can do this either verbally, or by means of a questionnaire. If you decide to have them fill out a questionnaire, it's probably wise to link it to some sort of competition. Get them to fill it out and then drop it back into a box for the chance to win a prize. The more worthwhile the prize, the better the response you'll receive.

Finding out which station your customers prefer will assist you in deciding which station to have playing in your store. Whilst you may not like the music they play, the customer is after all the person you're trying to satisfy.

Step 4: What (Do You Want To Say To Your Prospects)?

There's often heated debate about which type of radio commercials work best, but there's never a disagreement about which type don't. Those with no obvious purpose fail every time.

For example, if your commercial says 'Hi, my name's John. I mow lawns and I've been doing it for 12 years,' it's unlikely to get people to call. Your commercial needs to give people a good reason to listen, then a great reason to take action. Either they must call you or come into your store.

Your commercial needs to have a clear purpose and take people from point A to point B. Point A is your opening, which should identify a benefit, need or dissatisfaction they're currently experiencing in their lives. The second part of the commercial leads them to Point B, which is where you tell them why they should act right now and how to do it.

Most important is understanding your customers. If you understand their needs, wants and current position, you can sell them almost anything.

For example, having a commercial which said, 'Attention all men who suffer from impotence. Here's how you can be cured with just one simple phone call,' would probably bring an excellent response. Or a commercial aimed at teenagers, which said, 'Forget the fake ID ... here's how you can get access to Sydney's best nightclubs before your 18th.'

These commercials reach out and speak to your audience. If you don't understand the people you're aiming your commercial at, you'll inevitably fail to get a response from your advertising. Imagine running a commercial aimed at housewives that said, 'Here's how you can put more fun into your ironing.' The listeners would be downright confused and probably furious as the last thing they want to think about is doing the ironing.

Before writing your commercial, you need to decide exactly what message you want to communicate. Then you need to decide what you want your audience to do. In other words, what action do you want them to take?

Here's a great example. John, the lawn mowing professional, decides to write a new commercial. Considering the abysmal result of his previous 'Hi, my name's John' commercial, he resolves to get more specific. This time he has a clear message. You see, he has a new automatic re-booking system that makes life easier and saves his customers 20%. He also has a specific objective. He wants to encourage his customers to use the new system and book a cut within the next two weeks. Now the campaign has a good chance of working.

It pays to remember that simply asking people to act now is rarely enough. You need to give them a good reason why NOW is the time to do something. You see, most purchases can be delayed forever. It's one thing to create desire, but it's another to actually get people to part with their cash. Every month customers have to decide what to spend their money on. Every buyer has priorities. Of course, there are ways to re-arrange these priorities. That's the challenge business owners face.

The question is, how do you offer a great deal without slicing your profit margin drastically? There's a couple of ways. First, make sure you're selling products or services with a high margin. Often, that's not possible but remember, it's much easier to come up with great deals if you can. If you can't, you need to find items or services that are highly valued by your customers, yet have a low cost. Extra service is an old standby, information booklets are another. Even better are services you can get for free from other businesses. For example, a hairdresser could offer to introduce their clients to a beauty salon if the beauty salon agrees to give customers a free facial.

Step 5: How (To Write A Commercial That Works)?

It's a common misconception that you have to be a great writer, or some wizard with words, to write a commercial that works.

That's rubbish. People who simply know the people they're targeting, and know how to come up with a good offer write many of the most successful commercials. Their writing skills are irrelevant.

Simply running a commercial aimed at new homeowners saying, 'Here's how you can cut eight years off your mortgage ... guaranteed. We're currently offering a FREE introductory session to the first 14 callers. This session is normally valued at $145,' is enough. It doesn't matter what language you use, or even if your commercial poorly produced.

It's the message that's important

At the end of the day, it can't be said people will buy from you just ~
write witty commercials a standup comic would be proud of. ~
people probably won't avoid buying from you, because your ~
if it was produced on Aunt Laura's $25 petrol-driven tape ~

As long as your message is clear, quick and targe~
work. It's really like serving food: if you are servin~
good delivered on paper plates as it will on yo~
the silver, but if you're serving to people ~
eat anyway.

There is only one sin you don't ~
or rambling on too long. If ever ~
to the sale, fine. If your ~
very quickly.

The same applies if you s~
some guidelines for creating a ~

Number Of Words Per Commercial

As a rule 65 - 85 words is the limit for a 30 second commercial. This can vary, however, depending on the style of commercial and how many sound effects you use. One of the most common mistakes people make when writing their own commercial, is putting too many words in and then trying to make them fit.

To check you haven't got too much in your ad, read it out aloud and then time it as you read. When reading a commercial you need to speak only marginally faster than normal speed. Whilst it's possible to read 100 words in 30 seconds by talking very fast, you're better off cutting down on the words and making it easier to understand.

It's important you realise radio is a background medium. Most people listen to it while doing something else such as driving or working in the garden. Understand it's important not to put too much information into your ads.

You should only focus on one theme; the one 'big idea' you want to get across. Trying to explain something that's complex or detailed is a recipe for disaster when advertising on radio. While listing benefits is important in any form of advertising, it's best to just focus on the one that consumers will find most appealing.

Opening Lines

As I've just mentioned, radio is a background medium. As a result you need to get your prospect's attention immediately. A simple way of doing this is simply by telling them whom it is you're talking to. For example, if your commercial is aimed at business people, you could do worse than having an opening line that says, "Attention Business People."

Using the key benefit of your product or service is another great way of getting your target's attention. When looking for the benefit, you quite often need to identify a problem people would like a solution to. Once you've discovered what they're dissatisfied with, your opening lines virtually write themselves.

To demonstrate this, let's look at an earlier example. Remember how we looked at the problems involved with a commercial that said, "Here's how you can put more into your ironing." Imagine the same commercial with an opening line that says, "Here's how you can cut your ironing time in half." Do you think this would spark interest?

Another way to approach your opening line is to invoke curiosity. This is harder to do but better if your product doesn't contain a striking benefit. Here's an example. "Here's why three out of four Auckland children will lose their hair by 2015." Or "Four reasons to call George's Gym before July 15 and say bye-bye to flab-owee."

Most importantly, your opening line needs to stop the listener dead in their tracks. Another trick is to start your commercial off as if it were an important announcement. For example, "We interrupt our regular programming for this important news flash." This is a great way to attract your prospect's attention. It can be even more powerful if the start of your commercial is the opening few bars of a popular song, and you then interrupt it.

Finding The Right Voice For Your Commercial

This can be more important than you might realise. The wrong voice can severely hamper the result your commercial achieves. By taking some time to make this decision, your commercial will have a much greater chance of success. You may be tempted to voice the commercial yourself. However, unless you have a good voice for radio, you're better off getting someone else to do this for you. This can cause problems for some people, especially those who only chose this form of advertising so they could hear their own voice on the radio.

Understand that the reason you're using radio is to get results, not to massage your own ego. There is, however, an exception to this rule. By using the 'we're local' appeal, you may be able to get the edge over your 'new to town' opposition. And yes, I know I said the quality of production isn't as important as what you say, but why not have the best of both worlds?

You need to keep in mind who you're trying to reach and the type of person they'll find believable. You'll benefit greatly by finding a voice your target market can relate to. To demonstrate how important this is, imagine using a male voice to talk about period pain. Or having a lady voicing a commercial for impotence. Using the wrong voice can detract from the credibility of your commercial.

You can always request a local announcer voices your commercial. This will normally be done free of charge if you're running the commercials on their radio station. This can be beneficial if the announcer has a strong following and good credibility among your target market. If you decide to use a local announcer, keep in mind they probably won't be able to use terms such as us and we. If you want the reader to sound like a representative of your company, you may need to source outside talent.

Using Music

Should you choose to have music in your commercial, there are a number of things to consider. Firstly, what type of music do your potential clients enjoy? If you're aiming at an older age group, you'll need to use the type of music they grew up with. It would be detrimental to the effectiveness of a campaign aimed at 50 years olds to have rap style music in your ad. Of course, this would be ideal if you're targeting people aged 20 or under.

Radio Campaign

You also need to consider the type of music played by the station you're using. Of course, the type of music the station plays will generally be the type of music your target market prefers to listen too. If it isn't, they'd probably change stations.

Because the majority of people who listen to radio do so for the music, It's a good idea to include it in your commercials. If you're aiming at a younger age group, the more modern the music, the more effective the ad. By making the start of your commercial sound like a popular song, you increase the chances of people paying attention to it.

You do need to be careful about which music you use. Copyright laws will cover some songs and instrumentals, particularly those that haven't been around long. To ensure you're not in breach of these laws, you should check with your radio station representative. You may still be able to use the music even if it is protected, providing you pay a royalty fee. These fees can be quite expensive however, so generally you're better off choosing a song not subject to royalty fees.

Using Sound Effects

People have so many things continuously competing for their attention. To ensure they notice your commercial, you need to make sure it has impact. One of the most effective ways to do this is by using sound effects.

There are literally thousands of options to choose from in this area, but there are a few fundamental points you need to consider when choosing the right ones. When considering the type of sound effect to use, ask yourself this: "If I had the radio on while driving or doing some other task, what sort of noise or effect would make me stop and take notice?"

When you consider your answer to this question, it's a good idea to get a clear mental image of the types of sounds you would normally hear on that station. People are attracted to loud or unusual sounds. If the sound effect you choose is the type not normally heard on that station, there's a good chance your commercial will make people sit up and take notice.

The effect you use also needs to suit the mood you're trying to create or the product you're trying to sell. For example, if you were trying to promote a nightclub, you'd probably use the sound of people laughing and having a good time in the background. If, however, you were trying to promote the fact that your retail store was busy, you'd still use the sound of a lot of people in the background, but instead of laughter, they'd sound busy and purposeful.

Understand that for the nightclub, you want to promote a fun and relaxed atmosphere. For the retail store however, you'd want to create a sense of urgency, a feeling of 'I'd better hurry or the stock will be gone before I get there.'

The right effect can also assist you in creating the right mood for your commercial. You would probably use loud exaggerated noises if you wanted to create humour in your ad.

On the other hand, if you were doing a commercial for a business that assists the victims of violence, you'd use more subtle, disturbing sound effects. Try to identify the mood you want before choosing the effect to go with your commercial.

Where to place the sound effects and how loud to have them are two more things you need to think long and hard about. There is no hard and fast rule about placement. It's entirely up to you whether you use them just at the start, in the middle, at the end, or all the way through your commercial.

Something else to consider when you're looking at where to place them is their ability to add disturbing impact to your ad. For example, imagine a commercial for a brake company which started with a women screaming and the sound of a car crash, followed by a moment of silence ...

Careful sound effects placement can create a powerful impression.

As to how loud your sound effects should be, once again it's pretty much up to you. There are some things you need to keep in mind, though. A particularly loud and annoying noise that goes on for a long period of time may result in people turning the radio off. Whilst it's a good idea to use a loud noise at the start of a commercial, it shouldn't interfere with your prospect's ability to understand what you're saying. You need to make sure your selling message is not drowned out by the sound effects. Try making the initial noise loud, but then fade it out as the presenter starts to speak.

As I mentioned earlier, there are literally thousands of effects from which to choose. Most major radio stations will have a library of effects that should contain the one you're after. If they don't have exactly what you need, they can either source it from another station, or possibly even create it for you. Once again your local radio sales person can assist you here.

Call To Action

Always include a strong, specific call to action. If you don't tell people what to do, they probably won't do anything. Give them precise instructions; who to call, which number to use, when to do it and what to ask for. Here's a good example: "Call Gordon Harris now on 3345 6756 and ask for your 45 page personal astrological analysis chart."

By putting a time limit on your offer or sale, you can create a sense of urgency. If people have to act fast to take advantage of a particular offer, guess what? They will. Make it very clear what it is you want them to do.

Radio Campaign

You also need to understand that because radio is a background medium, people probably won't have time to remember your phone number. Try giving them your address or perhaps a nearby landmark they may be familiar with. If you have to use a phone number, repeat it at least three times to give listeners a chance to remember it. Mention it early on in your ad, then again in the middle and finally at the end of your ad. By doing this, you're alerting people to the fact they need to be ready to either memorise the number or write it down. You might like to make your phone number the central theme of your commercial. By using your number as a rhyme, or part of a challenge (If you can recite this number, you'll get a free XYZ), you can increase the likelihood of listeners remembering it. Another technique you can use if you need people to call rather than come in to your store is to tell them to look your number up in the phone book.

Concise Copy

Include concise and convincing copy. Remember, the copy is the actual words between the introduction and the call to action.

You don't need to be a great writer to do this part well. It's more important you get the point across clearly, in as few words as possible, and in logical order.

After you write your first draft, go through and edit viciously. Cut out any sentence or word that doesn't need to be there. Remember, you can only use between 65 and 85 words in total, and this includes your introduction and call to action.

Next, read it aloud and make sure it flows. Time it as you read to make sure it will comfortably fit into 30 seconds. Lastly, have a couple of people check it through and ask them to tell you what they understood from it. Ask them to explain it back to you, just to make sure you're getting your point across. Ask which parts were boring, and don't be afraid of the criticism. You didn't set out to be the world's greatest writer anyway, so any comments should be helpful, rather than hurtful.

Avoid anything that's hard to comprehend. Write your commercial in a way that's easy for the consumer to understand. If your offer is long and complex, people won't be able to grasp it, and they won't respond.

Remember, people aren't interested in playing games by trying to decipher what it is you're trying to say. They just want to know if they should bother listening, and if they like what they hear, what they should do.

Don't make things confusing. It'll only obscure your message. Avoid being an artist. Be a business person.

Step 6: When (To Run Your Campaign)

If your product is perennial (that is, not seasonal), you don't have to be too concerned about when to run your commercials. It's more a question of which day, rather than which time of year.

If you're trying to attract business clients, it's usually a good idea to run your ads on Tuesday or Wednesday. People are usually feeling too busy on Monday, and pretty uninterested in thinking about anything new on Friday.

If, on the other hand, your business is seasonal, you need to approach your radio campaign slightly differently. For example, a sports store wouldn't run a campaign promoting cricket gear in the off-season. The business owner would need to adapt the appeal to suit the time of year. For example, they would rather promote rugby gear instead.

You also need to consider the placement of your commercials. This means the times you want them to go to air. There are two basic types of schedules you can choose from.

The first is referred to as 'run of station'. This simply means the station will decide when your commercials go to air, or in other words, the specific time of the day each will be played. Whilst this is the cheapest option, it's certainly not the best. If your commercials are placed 'run of station,' they will basically be used as fillers during unsold air time. That is, the time slots that nobody else wanted. Under this system your commercials could be played early in the morning when nobody is listening, or during other quiet times such as mid-afternoon. You can occasionally get lucky using this system, but you'll waste a lot of money if you don't.

The second type is 'target placed'. Using target placed commercials gives you the opportunity to decide when each commercial is played. This method is more expensive, but you also get to decide when your commercials will be played. This greatly improves the chances of them being heard by the right people. Your local station will have survey figures that indicate the most popular listening times for your potential customers. You need to find out which are the highest ? hour listening shares for your target demographic and then pay for your commercials to be played during those times. As I've already mentioned, this can be more expensive, but there's no point having your ads played at a time when your target market is not listening. Your station sales representative can tell you which times will suit you best.

Step 7: What Else (Do You Need To Think About)?

Use this section as a final checklist. Once you're happy with your commercials, run through them to make sure you're ready to get started. Here are a few things you may not have thought about:

Team Training

Does your team fully understand the strategy you've implemented? It's important they understand the vital role they are to play in this strategy. If new customers come in and find your service levels to be less than expected your radio campaign will fail.

Check Stock And Team Levels

It's unlikely your Radio campaign will bring in hundreds of people all at once (very few actually do), but you nevertheless need to be prepared for a sizeable response. There would be nothing worse than having a rush of new customers, only to find you have no stock or are to busy to serve them. Plan for your Radio campaign by making sure you can cater for any increased demand that may result.

Having considered this, you also need to be mindful of certain myths radio sales people would have you believe.

One of my favourites is that of **image advertising**. This is a tactic used to get you to spend vast sums of money without being able to gauge the effectiveness of your commercials. Your advertising dollars should only be spent on specific promotions, services or products. This allows you to test and measure the results.

Package deals and **special promotions** are another method they use to milk money out of the unsuspecting business owner. This typically occurs late in the month when the station is behind on budget. These can sometimes be worthwhile, providing your commercials are aired at a time that suits you and not simply placed run of station.

11 'Killer' Commercials

So, you understand the number of words you can use in a 30-second commercial. You also know how to effectively use music and sound effects to add impact to your ads.

Let's now take a look at 11 different 'types' of radio commercials, any one of which may suit your product or service.

Picture This

Using words and sound effects, you create a mental picture in the mind of the listener. This type of commercial clearly demonstrates a common problem and the way your product or service can provide a solution to it.

For example: **A commercial for a car breakdown service.**

The commercial starts off with the sound of a car that won't start. A man and a woman get into an argument because they'll be late for a party. A voice then explains that if they were a member of Joe Bloggs' breakdown service, they'd still have made the party on time. The commercial then cuts back to the couple who are still arguing.

Build A Character

This style of commercial develops a character who then becomes synonymous with your company. It's particularly effective if you're running an ongoing campaign, highlighting different areas of your business.

For example: **A character to promote an air-conditioning company.**

With the sounds of cattle and chickens in the background, an old farmer starts talking about problems on the land. He complains about the dry weather, the stock looking thin and generally miserable. He then goes on to say that the only good thing to happen down his way is XYZ air-conditioning services. He then mentions the price and the fact that now he's cool, he doesn't care when it rains. This character could then also do the opposite in winter, when promoting reverse cycle air-conditioning. Other suitable characters could be people with Scottish, American or Pakistani accents.

Use An Exaggeration

While this style can be quite humorous, it can also be very effective in communicating the key benefit of your product or service. This has the advantage of having consumers associate your product with that benefit.

For example: **Promoting a new hairdryer.**

A lady explains she has having trouble drying her hair with her old worn out hairdryer, which is simply not powerful enough. She then starts talking about the new hairdryer she brought from YYY retail store. The listener hears hurricane sound effects as she switches it on.

Radio Campaign

You could use this type of exaggeration to emphasise the speed of a new computer that types letters before people think of what to write. Or a mechanic who has your beat-up old Kingswood sounding like a Rolls Royce.

This type of commercial has unlimited applications.

Use A Familiar Theme Or Character

Another way to make your commercial stand out is to use the theme music to popular TV shows or movies. You can also use the characters from these shows.

For example: **A new range of homes.**

Using music from an old Western movie, a voice that sounds like John Wayne starts lecturing his housemates. He explains the home they're in at the moment isn't big enough for the all of 'em'. He then explains that by building a new home with Joe Bloggs Builders they can all live comfortably.

You can adapt this style of commercial to most businesses. How about the theme music and characters from Mission Impossible or Star Wars. With a little thought and effort, you could soon identify a theme for your company's radio campaign.

Be A Bit Suggestive

This is one of the more interesting ways to get your commercial noticed. Make it sound as if there's something naughty going on, using suggestive words, music and/or sound effects. Make sure you don't get carried away and miss the point. You need to still get across the key benefit, and it has to relate to the commercial itself.

For example: **Promoting a new bedding store.**

The commercial starts with a man and women grunting and groaning in the bedroom. He asks her to slide it in gently while he holds her end. The moaning then gets louder and louder until finally she says, "I give up, we're never going to get this sheet to fit." An announcer then comes on and explains that if you need new sheets, you should go and see ZXY Bedding.

Use Humour

Fun ads tend to be the most popular. But care should be taken when taking a humorous approach. The idea of running the campaign is to sell goods or services, not to make people laugh. This style of commercial is more suited to inexpensive items, as most expensive purchases are not considered a laughing matter. It can, however, be very effective for tradesmen.

For example: **Advertising a plumbing service.**

As the commercial begins we can hear a man grunting as he goes to the toilet, at a party. You then hear the sound of toilet paper being used, just as someone knocks on the door to tell him to hurry up because everyone's queuing up waiting to go. He tells them he's almost finished, and you hear him try to flush the toilet. He then realises to his horror that the toilet won't flush. An announcer then comes on promoting Joe Bloggs' Plumbing Services. The end line could be something like: "So call Joe today. He'll make those nasty little problems go away."

Make It Sound Like An Emergency Phone Call

Most people are familiar with the sound of an emergency phone call. This style can be either serious, or tongue-in-cheek. The key is to have the person who's making the call sound flustered, just as they would in real life.

For example: **A commercial promoting a First Aid course.**

The commercial begins with a frantic voice asking the emergency operator how to resuscitate a friend. The operator then tries to calmly talk the caller through the procedure. The caller then begins to cry, saying she can't do it, as she doesn't know what to do. You continue hearing the saga being played out as a voice comes over explaining that if the caller had done the XYZ First Aid Course, she would have been able to save her friend's life. The commercial finishes with the caller sobbing uncontrollably because her friend won't start breathing.

Telephone Talk Back

Here you make your commercial sound like a radio talk back program. The announcer introduces the next caller, whom he asks to speak about today's topic. The caller then goes off on a tangent explaining the benefits of a particular product or service. This is a very common strategy, but one that can work well for the right sort of business.

For example: **A new clothing store.**

The announcer starts off by saying, "And our next caller is Sally from Mitchem. Sally, do you think the Prime Minister has an image problem?" A female voice then says she does think so and that he should address it by getting his clothes from XYZ Clothing Boutique. The announcer tries to get her back on track, but she goes on to list the benefits of dealing with that particular store.

People Being Interviewed On The Street

Once again, this can be used as a serious or humorous type of commercial. Perhaps the most effective way of using it is by actually interviewing people and getting them to give you testimonials. Organise with your local radio station to get somebody to come to your store when it's busy. Then ask them to go around and interview your customers. This works well because most people like the idea of being on the radio, and will give your store a huge plug. Then simply pick the best of these and use them as your commercial.

For example: **A new food store.**

The announcer says, "We're here at XYZ Cafe Restaurant to find out what it is that makes people come here." He then goes on to interview people who comment on the great quality and range of food, the atmosphere and the service. The announcer then explains where the store is and what its trading hours are.

Radio Serials

You might like to try making your commercial sound like an old time radio serial. Using phrases and terms that were common from that era as well as the type of voices and characters that were around then, can make an outstanding commercial. The production department of the radio station can generally make your commercial sound a bit scratchy as well, just to add authenticity.

For example: **A new fast food, home delivery service.**

An old army major is talking to his friend about what he'd like for dinner. He mentions he'd like bacon. His friend replies, "Yes Sir, I'll just go and get that for you." A door closes in the background and immediately opens again. The friend, out of breath, says he's got the bacon. The Major then adds he'd like some tomato sauce. The friend replies, "Yes Sir, I'll just go and get that for you." And so it goes on until the major says, "For goodness sakes man, you could've just called XYZ Pizza Delivery." He then explains that they have inexpensive home deliveries with a choice of toppings. As you can see, having a line, which is repeated over and over, makes the commercial more effective. This was a common theme with earlier radio serials.

People Talking On Telephones Or CB Radios

The reason for the success of this style of commercial is that people are used to hearing people on the phone without being able to see them. This is the same with radio advertising, as you can hear people but you can't see them. Two ladies talking on the phone about a new shop that's opened, or two policemen talking about a new car that just went past, are some examples of how this can be used effectively.

For example: **A new gymnasium.**

A lady comments to her friend about the amount of weight Michele Smith has lost. The other lady says she must be starving herself. As the two make catty remarks about Michele, an announcer comes over to explain you can now lose all the weight you want at XYZ Gymnasium.

These are just 11 examples of the types of radio commercials from which you can choose. You may have noticed that up until now I haven't mentioned jingles. This is because unless you have an enormous budget, jingles are a waste of money. Large companies like Coca-Cola and McDonalds, who pour millions of dollars each year into advertising, use jingles to good effect. But for the average business, your money is better spent on specific promotions.

"So Charlie, how did you go?"

"Great Brad. You were right. This is really fun. You can let your imagination run wild, can't you?"

"That's exactly right, Charlie. I can tell you have some ideas for your own radio commercial already."

"You're not wrong, mate. Listen, this is what I'm going to do."

He picked up his pencil and began writing furiously, mumbling to himself every now and then. After a while, he leaned back in his chair, pushed his cap onto the back of his head and wiped his forehead with the back of his other arm. He looked pleased with himself.

"Here, tell me what you think of this."

Here's Charlie's First Radio Commercial:

*** Radio Copy ***

Title: Charlie's Garage Tyre Deal

Requested Talent (1): (Male) (Age: 40+)
Requested Talent (2): (None)
Requested Talent (3): (None)

Length: 00:45

Campaign Start Date: (20/11/96)
Campaign Finish Date: (27/11/96)
Station: (2YZ – FM)

—————————————————————Copy Text————————————————————

SFX:	(Whip cracking and cows mooing)
VOICE (1):	(Cowboy accent) Yeehah!
VOICE (1):	It's Sheriff Charlie here, back in town lookin' to lynch crook tyres.
VOICE (1):	Now we all know that crook tryes are killers. So I'm offerin' up a reward for anyone who rustles up a couple of varmints.
VOICE (1):	If you run in two or more crook tyres, I'll give you $20 towards the cost of your new tyres.
VOICE (1):	So mosey in on now to Sheriff Charlie's Garage, corner Smith and Dominion Road.
VOICE (1):	And help me lynch those crook tyres.

Examples

So now its time to see how all these elements come together. In this section I'll show you two examples of radio commercials that are designed to stand out from the rest. After you've gone through them, go back over your notes and try your hand at creating your own radio commercial. It's easy and it's fun.

*** **Radio Copy** ***

Title: XYZ Copiers

Requested Talent (1): Announcer – Mike Smith
Requested Talent (2): (Boy) (Age: 10)
Requested Talent (3): (Girl) (Age: 10)

Length: 00:30

Campaign Start Date: (20/11/96)
Campaign Finish Date: (27/11/96)
Station: (2YZ – FM)

——————————————————Copy Text——————————————————

VOICE (2):   My nan and pop live a long way away!

VOICE (3):   Mine live further!

VOICE (2):   Well, mine are very sad because they don't get to see me very much …

VOICE (3):   Mine see me every day …

VOICE (2):   How?

VOICE (3):   Mum had a photo of me put on a calendar from XYZ Copiers, so they can see me whenever they want.

VOICE (2):   Well, I'm going to tell my mum about this …

VOICE (1):   XYZ Copiers, 432 Smith Street.

2 voices and SFX.

*** **Radio Copy** ***

Title: (Insert your title here)

Requested Talent (1): (Announcer/Male/Female) (Age: 00)
Requested Talent (2): (Male/Female) (Age: 00)
Requested Talent (3): (None)

Length: 00:30

Campaign Start Date: (00/00/00)
Campaign Finish Date: (00/00/00)
Station: (Insert station name here)

―――――――――――――――――Copy Text―――――――――――――――――

SFX: (Insert relevant sound effects here)

VOICE (1):   (Insert copy here)

VOICE (2):   (Insert copy here)

VOICE (1):   (Insert copy here)

VOICE (2):   (Insert copy here)

VOICE (1):   (Insert copy here)

SFX

VO :   Insert your location and contact details here.

SFX

he second most important element is the headline. You'll also discover how to
te effective headlines shortly.

nother important consideration is whether to make an offer or not, and if you
e, just what you should be offering. No matter how well written your
dvertisement is, a great offer can get your phone running hot.

In the following pages, you'll learn how to write headlines that work, how to
osition your photographs for maximum impact and which typefaces have the best
recognition rates. You'll also discover what size you should use and which benefits,
angles and appeals work best.

The 5 Steps To Yellow Pages Success

Step 1: Who (Is Your Target Market)?

If you don't know who your target market is, it's almost impossible to attract their
attention. You need to know as much about them as possible. Their characteristics
are known as demographics by industry professionals. These facts are gathered
rough pain-staking market research studies, and are available if you know where to
k. The Australian Bureau of Statistics also conducts annual research into every
ct of the Australian population, and their findings are made public on an on-
basis.

mber, if you don't know whom you are trying to reach through advertising,
eally just taking your chances. That certainly doesn't make much
ense.

specific - who are the people most likely to be interested in your product
ow old are they? Are they male or female? How much do they earn and
live? Are they ready to buy? Remember, people looking in the Yellow
to buy – they just need to know who to buy from. If you win their
probably win their business.

Do You Want To Say)?

g as image advertising, especially in the Yellow Pages. Forget
ed to do is say something to your potential readers. Your
nvey a strong message. This may be in the form of an offer,
ifference or a list of the benefits they'll get from dealing

Part 3

▌Yellow Pages

"Charlie, now that we've taken care of Classified Advertising and Radio Commercials, we'll have a closer look at what's involved in compiling an advertisement for the Yellow Pages. You see, the Yellow Pages is a great cost-effective place to advertise for businesses like yours."

"That's great, Brad. I guess we could just use our Classified Ad, couldn't we?"

"Yes and no. You see, there are some specific things that make the Yellow Pages different from your local paper. But we'll get to that in a moment. Let's go back basics for the moment, shall we?"

"No worries, Brad. I can't wait to find out more, because if I know you, be things I would never have thought about …"

What Is A Successful Advertisement?

Advertising in the Yellow Pages is, in essence, no diff anywhere else. Except, perhaps, they're a dicey prospect fr ad will run for a whole year, whether it works or not. effectiveness either, aside from placing ads in smaller them in the paper as well. Both of these meth though; they are not parallel situations. Even exceptionally well in either of these medium Pages too. So, getting back to our questi

Basically any advertisement that pa not to say our objective is to spe of it. There is such a thing as l spend with you over the co focus on bringing the cust that covers its cost init

What Make

There ar
advertisement

Position is numbe
do to influence this. You

lo
asp
goin

Rem
you're
business

So let's g
or service.
where do the
Pages are read
attention, you'l

Step 2: What

There's no such thi
about it. What you m
Yellow Pages ad must c
an important point of
with you.

It's essential WHAT you say is appealing to WHOM you are trying to say it to. For example, throwing in a bungee jump with enrolment at a retirement village probably won't work. A free celebration dinner with the elderly person's children and grandchildren might.

Let's deal with each type of message, one by one.

Listing The Benefits

If you don't have a strong offer or point of difference, listing the benefits to be gained from dealing with you may do the trick. For example, a hairdresser could list the four reasons they give the best haircuts in town, or a beauty salon could emphasise the six ways a prospect's skin will improve after only one visit.

Most importantly, you must relate the benefits to the customer. Remember; always write your ad about their favourite subject – THEM.

Point Of Difference

This can work well when there is a large market for your product, as well as many competitors. For example, if you were advertising a 'steak and seafood' restaurant, you'd be hard pressed to stand out. But what if your steakhouse had live entertainment, free drinks from 7pm and the best view in town? Now that would be worth promoting.

Biggest & Best

This is where you simply go for the biggest ad, have the biggest words and answer every commonly asked question. Your text could be as simple as, 'we're cheap, fast, experienced and always open.'

Strong Offer

Remember, people are ready to buy when they read the Yellow Pages. A small incentive on top can really take it over the top. Be realistic though. If you don't have a strong offer, it's probably not worth the trouble shouting about it as nobody will ever mention it. An ad with an offer that stops them in their tracks can really work. Read more about offers in Part 10.

Have another read through these options, then choose the one you think best suits your business. For example, if you have something that has a high-perceived value yet a low cost to you, the offer approach could be the one for you. If there's something different about you, you should emphasise it.

Step 3: How (To Write Your Advertisement)

Now that we've covered the basics, it's time to get to the fun part of how to write your Yellow Pages ad.

Headline

Using a strong a headline can easily double your response rate. To understand why, think about this situation. You're shopping for air conditioning in the Yellow Pages. The first ad you look at has 'George's Cool World' in big letters up the top. The second says, 'Air-conditioning City.' The third has a headline that says, '7 reasons to call Harry's Air-conditioning.'

Which one are you more likely to read?

Generally, adding a headline is like creating a breath of fresh air in your section. Whilst everybody else is so intent on putting their business name in ultra-large type, you'll actually be providing people looking with a reason to read your ad.

Here are some great examples of Yellow Pages headlines that will help your ad stand out.

"7 reasons to call Jim's Widgets first."

"DON'T call anyone for Widget's until you read this."

"6 reasons why I'm the best Widget supplier on this page."

"4 things that are different about Jim's Widgets."

"Advice for those looking for Widgets."

"Warning ... don't buy Widgets until you've read this."

Each of these headlines can be applied to any business in any section. And each one has been proven to blow the other ads off the page.

It's also important to remember that people are looking to buy – so treat them that way. You don't have to convince them that buying your type of product or service is a good idea. You need to persuade them to buy from YOU.

Include a headline that reflects that idea. One other thing – the headline needs to take up at least 25% of your advertisement.

Sub-Headlines

Sub-headlines have three major benefits:

They break up large blocks of text making them easier to read. If your advertisement looks like one big 'chunk' of text it can put people off reading it. By using sub-headlines you can break your copy up and give it some space.

- They allow someone skimming over your ad to only read the points that interest them.
- They spark the reader's interest. If your headline doesn't get them in completely, you can get a second chance with your sub-headlines.

It is important your sub-headlines tell a story. They need to be able to convey your message to those who are just browsing over your ad.

Body Copy

You only get one chance with a potential customer, so your first 50 words are crucial. You must arouse your reader's curiosity immediately, with the very first paragraph. If they're not excited after the first 50 words they won't read the rest of your ad.

Use the bare minimum of copy to get your message across. Never waffle on. But make sure you include enough information to get your reader interested enough to call. You should never tell the whole story in your ad. You probably won't have enough space in any event. Tell them as much as you need to. By holding back some information you make it necessary for them to call you to find out more.

Your ad should tell a story and be easy to read. When you finish writing it, get someone to look it over and critique it for you. Only make one offer in your ad but make it an exciting one.

Keywords

One of the most important things to know about Yellow Pages advertising is that people are looking for keywords.

Here's an example:

Let's say you're after someone to re-tile your bathroom. You're looking for two words – tiling and bathroom. If you see an ad with those two words somewhere in it, you'll call the number.

On the other hand, if the ad simply says 'all tiling jobs,' you may not call. People need to be completely sure they're dialing someone who can provide what they want. If the ad doesn't specifically mention what they're looking for, there's a chance they'll pass it by.

Think about the words your target market is looking for. If you rent appliances, it pays to mention everything you rent in the ad, not just 'all appliances.' In large type, write 'fridges, TV's, videos, washing machines' and so on. Include everything.

Remember, the objective is not necessarily to be the best ad on the page. It's just to get people to call. Including key words is a way to ensure this happens.

Use Pictures

Pictures are absolutely essential in every Yellow Pages ad. People see pictures before words, and they tend to translate them into thoughts immediately. For example, a picture of a Lamborghini in a car sales ad tells you this is a quality car yard. If you were after a quality car, you'd be instantly attracted to this ad. If you're after something a little cheaper, you might look at the ad with the picture of the 1972 Datsun 200B.

Put a meaningful picture in your ad and you'll see your response skyrocket. For example, placing a picture of someone kicking a punching bag in a Kung Fu lessons ad will boost the number of calls massively. Or what about a person being massaged in a massage ad?

Don't try to be clever. Just use a picture of whatever it is that you're selling. If it's dogs, include a big picture of a dog. If it's security doors, show the designs you have. Another important point to remember is that people like to look at people. If you're including a picture of your product, make sure there's a person in the ad.

The reasoning behind this is simple. The first thing your eyes look for are other eyes.

Open up any page of the Yellow Pages and you'll discover this to be true. The first thing you'll see is the people.

It's also a good idea to put a picture of you in the ad. Aside from the fact that it attracts the eye, it also adds credibility. The logic is clear: people tend to think, "If they're willing to put their photo in the ad, they must be above board." And it's important to keep in mind that people don't buy from companies, they buy from other people.

People spend all their time interpreting pictures (that is, what they see) and only a small portion reading. Ensure you make your ad visually appealing. Studies have shown ads containing a picture that takes up between 25 - 75% of the total advertisement have greater readerships than those without one. Don't use line drawings or clipart. Photographs get a much higher response rate than illustrations. And always put a caption under your photograph. Everybody reads the captions so make sure you take advantage of this opportunity to get them into your ad.

Add A Definite Call To Action

Don't be wishy-washy with your ad. TELL people what you want them to do. There's nothing wrong with saying, in big bold letters, "Call George right now and organise a free consultation today."

Actually, it's 100% recommended that you put in something like that. There are three things that make a call to action work.

Firstly, you need to tell them when to act. As a general rule, NOW is the best time. Other options are today, immediately, or in rare cases, next time you …

Secondly, you need to tell them precisely how to communicate with you. Either drop in, call or fax. In Yellow Pages, the aim is to get them to phone you, and then to drop in.

Thirdly, you need to tell them what they are contacting you for. An appointment, a quote, more information, a free consultation or a tour of the showroom. Combined, your call to action might run like this: "Call now and ask to be sent a complimentary information package."

You might also like to include an offer as part of your call to action. For example, a free design consultation or a free voucher for a second dog wash when you have their first one (new customers only).

If They Zig, You Zag

If all the ads in your section look the same, you're very lucky. It'll be easy for yours to stand out.

If all the ads are full of text, adding a few pictures will work wonders. If they're all in colour, stick with plain black. If no one includes any detail, add a little more text to yours.

Anything that says, "Hey, I'm different to the other 12 ads on this page," is generally good. Of course, if there's something everyone's doing that undoubtedly works, do it too, but do it better. For example, if every ad has a guarantee, make yours longer, better and more powerful.

Whatever you do, ensure your ad stands out from the crowd.

Typefaces

The typeface or font you use in your advertisement can make a big difference to the results you achieve. The two basic types are Sans Serif and Serif fonts. Remember, Sans Serif fonts don't have the little "feet" at the bottom of each letter. They are more difficult to read.

The most common type of serif font is Times New Roman. Studies have also shown readership will not change if you use between 14 and 7 ? point size. But as a general rule, 10 or 12 points are ideal.

Highlighting Text

Use bold type to highlight key points in your body copy, headlines and sub-headlines.

Italics can also be used to highlight key areas of text, although it can be hard to read and should only be used sparingly. Never use all capitals. The only time you can use all capitals is in a short headline, or for extra emphasis.

To make your advertisement easier to read, break it up into paragraphs. Indenting your paragraphs, rather than leaving a line between them, can cut down on wasted space. Also consider using a drop cap first letter, as this is a great way to attract the eye of your next customer.

Location Guides

People are always looking for someone close by. For that reason, including your ad in a Location Guide can boost sales in a major way. But there is always the chance this can also work against you. You see, if people discount you because of your location, you'll never even get a chance to convince them you're worth the trouble. People will never look at your ad to begin with.

Step 4: How Big (Should Your Ad Be)?

Dependent on the sort of business you're in, going with a larger ad can make a lot of difference. Doubling the size of your ad will more than double your response. In fact, it has been proven that if you get 100 calls with a 1-unit display ad, you'll get 400 using a 2-unit ad. Going up to 4 units will boost response to 1100 calls.

Not only is it more likely your ad will be seen, you'll get a better position. The bigger ads get closer to the start of the section, and tend to have a much higher readership. To understand why that is, you just need to think about how people read the Yellow Pages. They generally open up to the first page in the section, scan the first few ads, and then call one.

Usually, they won't buy from the first one they call. It's human nature to shop around a little before making a decision. In all likelihood, they'll call another two before deciding to make an appointment or visiting the store.

The interesting thing is, most people will simply call a selection of the first dozen large ads they see. If they are still looking after that, they generally fall into one of four categories:

- They're after something highly specialised.
- They're detail-orientated people who like to do everything thoroughly.
- They're extreme price shoppers who'll call a dozen places just to save a couple of bucks.
- They just like dealing with the smaller guys.

There's nothing wrong with these shoppers, but they're the minority and sometimes harder to service. Unless you do something truly unique, it pays to go larger and deal with the masses.

Of course, the impact tends to be lost if everyone has a large ad. In that case, you need to do something else to stand out. Ultimately though, big is generally better, and more likely to bring you a good response.

But despite this, you do need to also keep in mind the cost vs. the likely outcome. For example, if your ad costs you $15,000 and your average profit on a sale is only $10, you'll need to make 1500 sales, or approximately 30 a day, from the Yellow Pages just to break even. If that's realistic, go for it. If it's not, re-consider. Perhaps your money is better spent elsewhere.

There's a lot more to working out the size your ad should be than most people think. Usually, it's simply a case of how much you can afford. The question should really be how much do you want to make?

If the ad is good enough, it should make you money, not drain your funds. If you don't have an ad that you know works, you'll need to guess. You need to think about how many responses you need to break-even. That means, how many sales do you need to pay back the advertising cost?

Step 5: What Else (Do You Need To Think About)?

Use this section as a final checklist. Once you're happy with your ad, run through and make sure you're ready to get started. Here are a few things you may not have thought about.

Production: For example, you may need to take some new photographs. Don't compromise here. People interpret a lot from photos; a bad one can really put them off.

If you want to ensure your ad appears exactly as you've intended, you may need to send Yellow Pages a bromide - talk to a printer about this if you're unsure. Also, make sure you check everything before it goes to print. Check your proof thoroughly. Don't let it go to print with spelling mistakes or the wrong phone number.

Phone Scripts: There are hundreds of cases where a Yellow Pages ad bought in so much business, yet meant very little at the end of the day because the business owner couldn't handle the response. How come? It's all comes down to how the prospect is handled by the business. Many stay just that – prospects, because they weren't converted into customers. To ensure this doesn't happen to your business, you need a script. This is nothing more than a version of what you say to encourage people to buy. Just think about the best sales lines you've ever used, and write them down. Make sure you ask lots of open-ended questions; you know, the one's that start with who, what, where, why or when. Give a copy of the script to every member of your team and make sure they USE it.

And of course, make sure your team knows an advertisement has been placed and to EXPECT calls. It doesn't matter how many calls you get. If you're blowing all the leads you get, you'll get nowhere.

Generally, most Yellow Pages enquiries run like this...

"Hello, Jim's Dog Washing."

"Hi, I'm just calling about the price of a dog wash."

"Yep, that's $10 for little dogs, $15 for big ones."

"Ok, I'll call you back."

"Ok, bye."

Do they ever call back? Rarely, and if they do, it's only because you're the cheapest. If it turns out there's someone else who's doing it for a few dollars less (and there always is), you'll lose out every time. Instead of giving your callers the price, try throwing this line at them:

"Thanks for your call. Just so I can help you best, would it be OK if I asked you a few questions?"

Nobody, and I mean NOBODY, will say, "No, just give me the price." In every case, they'll say, "Yeah, that's fine."

From here on in you're free to ask whatever you wish, leading them towards the sale. Taking the dog washing example, here's how the conversation could have gone:

"Hello, Jim's Dog Washing."

"Hi, just calling about the price on a dog wash."

"Thanks for you call. Just so I can help you best, would it be OK if I asked you a few questions?"

"Yeah, OK."

"Firstly, what sort of dog do you have?"

"German Shepherd."

"And your dog's name is?"

"Sweetie."

"Is Sweetie a fully grown dog, or just a pup?"

"He's pretty big."

"OK, have you had him washed before?"

"Only once, and that was about a year ago."

"Were you happy with the wash?"

"Not really, he ended up with fleas a couple of weeks afterwards, and the washers made a mess on my driveway."

"That's interesting – have you heard about our free flea and tick rinse we give with every wash?"

"No."

"We also have a guarantee to leave everything clean and tidy. Did you know about that?"

"Yeah, I saw something about it in your ad."

"When did you need your dog washed?"

"I don't know, some time this weekend."

"OK, I've got an appointment time free Saturday afternoon at 3pm, and one on Sunday at 11am. Which would suit you best?"

"Umm, Sunday I guess."

"OK, I'll be there at 10:55am. By the way, what's your address?"

Bit of a difference? And it's so simple – all you need to do is use the line and ask questions. You'll be amazed by how many more enquiries you convert to sales.

Check Stock And Team Levels: You need to be prepared for a sizable response. There's nothing worse than running a successful ad, only to run out of stock or being too busy to service these new enquiries. Plan ahead to make sure you can cater for any increased demand.

"Well, Charlie, we've covered a lot of ground. What are your feelings so far?"

Charlie leaned back in his chair, tilted his head back and stared at the ceiling, deep in thought. Slowly he straightened up and turned to face me, his eyes alight with excitement.

"I've got to tell you, Brad, this has been the best morning of my business life, that's for sure. I didn't realise just how simple, and powerful, all this business stuff really is. Man, I really should have been getting into this years ago. But never mind ..."

He was deep in thought again, and I didn't want to disturb him. Then he suddenly continued, "I've got a great idea for my Yellow Pages Ad. What do you think of this?"

At last ... A garage that promises no surprises!

No Surprises ... We'll tell you precisely what we're doing.

No Waiting ... We keep appointments – to the minute.

No High Prices ... You'll pay up to double if you go anywhere else. We are definitely the best value in the South-East. And we're the best.

Specialists in engine rebuilds, tune-ups, gearbox work, wheel alignment, restorations, air conditioning, brakes, steering, European and Japanese high performance cars, dyno tuning, turbo charging, electrical work and panelbeating.

Charlie's Photo

Charlie

Half Price Services - Guaranteed

Charlies Garage
Smith St, Smithville   **Ph: 1234 5678**

Here's Charlie's First Yellow Pages Advertisement:

Examples

Here are a few examples of successful Yellow Pages advertisements that have been designed with one thing in mind ... making sales.

Study them, keeping in mind what you've just learned. You'll notice how each one focuses on the key benefits.

You'll also notice each ad has a headline that delivers a selling message rather than just stating the company's name at the top. Look over these ads and refer back to them when writing your own.

Place Your Headline Here

Lorem et iusto odio dignissim qui blandit praesent luptatum zzril delenit au gue duis dolore te feugat nulla facilisi. Ut wisi enim ad orpersuscipit lobortis nisl ut aliqu ip ex en commodo consequat.

Address Here
Phone Fax

Place your Benefit Packed headline here ...

Place your sub-headline Here ...

Lorem et iusto odio dignissim qui blandit praesent luptatum zzril delenit au gue duis dolore te feugat nulla facilisi. Ut wisi enim ad orpersuscipit lobortis nisl ut aliqu ip ex en commodo consequat.

Duis te feugifacilisi.per. yj tyjk tyjkt rth yjetyjt. Jhb rg sfgn lobortis nisl ut aliqu ip ex en commodo dfg db consequat. Duis te feugifacilisi.per. yj tyjk dghmdgm.

*Place your
logo here*

Ph: 1234 5678

Your address and other details goes along here

*Place your
Photo here*

Part 4

▌ Host Beneficiary Relationships

It was now time to move on to some of the lesser known, but equally effective, lead generation strategies.

"What we're now going to consider, Charlie, is a strategy that can be so powerful it'll really get your business pumping."

"Better than what we've already gone through?"

"Oh yes. You see, get this right and you'll have other people doing your marketing for you. And not only that, you'll be spreading your wings in such a way that other businesses will love you. Let me explain what I mean."

The Nature Of Host Beneficiary Relationships

A host beneficiary relationship is one that exists when you and another business enter into a loose partnership to help each other make extra profits. For example, a hairdresser might offer a free style and cut to the database of a beauty salon. The hairdresser gets new clients, the beauty salon gets more customer loyalty and the customers appreciate the 'gift' from the beauty salon owner.

What Is A Successful Host Beneficiary Strategy?

The answer to this question is simple. If you make more money from it than it cost you, it's been a success. Basically, any Host beneficiary campaign that pays for itself can be considered successful.

But once again, before getting started, there are a few things you need to think about in depth.

Work Out Your Costs

This includes the cost of printing, envelopes, any implements you put into the envelope, phone calls, schmoozing with the other business owners, and anything else you can think of.

Host Beneficiary Relationships

Know Your Margins

You need to know the net profit you make from anyone who buys your product or service. By understanding how much you actually make from each sale, you'll be able to work out the percentage response required to make your campaign profitable.

Lifetime Value

Don't view each new customer your campaign brings in as a once-off sale. Remember you probably won't make money from your first sale to a new customer. Work hard on bringing them back at least 2 times.

What Makes A Successful Host Beneficiary Strategy?

Before I go into detail, there are a few things we need to get straight so we know what we're aiming for. To achieve this, I'll start by listing the main elements of a successful campaign.

The Right Attitude

One thing you'll discover from reading about host beneficiary strategies is you are doing the other business a favour as well. You need to understand they're getting as much benefit from it as you are.

Targeted Lists

You don't want to mail to anyone who would not be interested in your product or service. So you need to choose your host businesses carefully.

Offer

A strong offer will make all the difference. Without one, you can forget about response. With a powerful offer, you may need to hire extra staff just to cope with the fantastic response you could get.

Support From The Host

If your host business gets right behind the idea, you'll have a far better chance of success. If they go into it thinking, "Alright then, I don't like the idea but I'm willing to give it a try," you're fighting an uphill battle.

Phone Follow-Up

Unless you're selling directly off the page, you need to have an effective follow-up phone script. This can mean the difference between a 9% response rate, and one of 25%.

The 7 Steps To Creating Host Beneficiary Strategies

Step 1: Why (Use Host Beneficiaries)?

Before writing anything, you need to work out whether a host beneficiary strategy is for you. You need to compare its potential returns against other strategies to market yourself.

For example, if your market is broad and your offer is VERY appealing, why not use the newspaper instead? It's easier and probably a lot cheaper. Or what about radio?

Host beneficiary is ideal when you have a specific group of people you want to reach, and when there are other non-competitive businesses already dealing with them.

Here's a perfect example – corporate training organisations. They know who their target market is (businesses that need help with customer service and sales), and they both deal with other businesses like stationery suppliers and computer shops. A host beneficiary strategy could work here. The stationery supplier could send its customers a gift of a free 1-hour needs analysis with a qualified trainer.

On the other hand, a host beneficiary strategy is probably inappropriate for a fast food outlet. The market is probably too broad and it's hardly worth going through the trouble and expense of setting up a host beneficiary strategy. They may as well just put an ad in the paper as there's no specific business that would make a good host in this instance.

Remember, host beneficiaries work best because the potential customer thinks the offer is a gift from the other business. They believe the business has gone out of its way to find this offer, and to pass it on. Because of this, they feel some obligation to take it up. You need to find businesses that are willing to get behind the idea 100%, or else forget it.

This brings us to the other consideration: are there any businesses out there that are willing to open their minds up enough to run with the idea?

Of course, it all depends how you bring the idea up with them in the first place. If you say, "Listen, I want to use your database and sap it for all it's worth," you'll have a bit of a battle closing the 'sale.' On the other hand, you could try an approach

Like this: "Hi there, I've got a way we can help each other. I'll get some new customers, and your current customers will think you are the greatest, the most generous person on the planet. Then, later down the track, we'll swap." It's certain you'll get a better response from the second method.

Step 2: Who (Is Your Target Market)?

Before you even start making a list of potential host businesses, you need to identify exactly whom it is you're trying to reach. Precisely who is your target market?

A failure to answer this question will lead to failure FOREVER. For example, imagine a company that sells in-ground swimming pools doing a mailing campaign to a block of high-rise rental apartments. To avoid costly mistakes, you need to know who your potential customers are before you start arranging host beneficiaries with anyone.

Knowing your target market will also enable you to write in a way your prospect will relate to. Using terms and phrases that are commonly used by them will greatly increase the effectiveness of your letters to the customers of the host business.

So let's get specific. Who are the people most likely to be interested in your product or service? Here are some guidelines.

Age: How old are they? Think of an age that symbolises most of your customers.

Sex: Are they male or female? Which gender does business with you more often?

Income: How much do they make? It's essential that you find this out.

Where do they live: Are they local, or do they come from miles around to deal with you?

Step 3: Which (Business Will Make A Good Host)?

Now you've identified the 'who' you need to find the right business to help you reach them.

There are a number of criteria for selecting a host business. If you can think of one that matches each of these points, you're in business. If you can find a few that meet most of the criteria, it will probably still be worth running the strategy. Here's your checklist.

Non-Competitive

This means they don't sell what you sell, or anything that could be considered a replacement for what you sell.

For example, an acupuncturist and a masseuse may be considered competitive as both deal in natural therapy and relaxation. If customers start coming for a massage, they may stop seeing their acupuncturist.

There is such a thing as wallet share: customers have only so much to spend each month. If the masseuse becomes their choice for relaxation, the acupuncturist will miss out.

The same might go for a CD store and a video store. If people spend all their disposable income on CD's, they may have none left over for videos. It sounds crazy, but it's a genuine fact. People set aside a rough amount each month for a particular type of activity. If your business replaces the other business, you're competitive.

Of course, if you manage to get a semi-competitive business to promote you, then more power to you. It's their loss, not yours.

Usually, there's a lot of grey area here as it could be argued that all businesses are competitive in one way or another. Everybody wants the same type of customer; one with money to spend.

Some business owners are too paranoid to bother with. They think you're going to steal their customers. There's not much you can do about people like this. Just go for the ones with a good attitude.

Same Target Market

This is the most important consideration. The host business must have the same or a very similar target market to you.

For example, a high-class beauty salon and an exclusive hairdresser are very compatible, a Ford dealership and an auto-electrician specialising in Fords click well, as do a Hi-Fi shop and a CD store.

If you know who your target market is, you should have a clear idea of the people you want to target. You should know how old they are, how much they make, what they're interested in and more.

Now think about this. Who else deals with them? You can approach it from the other way – what other businesses do these people deal with? For example, members of a gym might also go to a health food store, or people who buy luxury cars might also like expensive paintings.

They Have A Database

You can't mail to anyone if the host business doesn't have the names and addresses of their customers.

Of course, it's not entirely essential, as you can ask the host business to simply hand envelopes to their customers, or make verbal recommendations. The latter tends to work less well.

Host Beneficiary Relationships

Ideally, find someone who has a computer database, or at the very least, one on paper. If their records are on paper, you could sweeten the offer to them by suggesting you will organise for their records to be transcribed onto computer. You see, if you're going to do it properly, you'll need to do this anyway, so why not throw it in.

Right Attitude

There's a heck of a lot of jaded business owners out there. They think the whole world is against them, the 'big boys' are discounting their prices to force them out of business and the economy's 'stuffed'.

These people are unlikely to go for anything any more complicated than flyers to letterboxes, which they'll tell you don't work anyway. If they are negative from the outset, you probably don't want to get too involved with them. They'll only kill your promotion.

It's better to find someone who's willing to give you the support you need. Someone who's smart enough to know a good business idea when they hear one. There are people out there like that, and they'll love to get involved.

Their Customers Like Them And They Like Their Customers

There are two things you don't want. The first is to mail to a hostile database that doesn't want anything to do with the host business. The second is to get a whole bunch of new customers who are essentially D-grade customers. You know, the ones that haggle on price, annoy the heck out of you and always complain about everything.

You need to check that the host business thinks highly of their customers. If they don't, you don't really want to adopt them as your own.

Big Database

If the host business only has 23 customers on it's list, it's barely going to be worth the trouble mailing to them (although this does depends on your business).

If they have a huge database, you may even want to offer exclusivity to the business in exchange for access to the whole list, including phone numbers. If they only have a small list, they can forget about exclusivity.

A Willingness To Test

It's important you stress to the host business you just want to do a small number first before mailing to everyone.

If the business owner says, "No, let's send them all out with our newsletter," it's a less than ideal situation. You really want to test first before doing the lot. It's also important your letter goes out alone, with no other material.

You could say to the host business owner, "I think we should do a hundred first, just to make sure everything's OK. I mean, of course it will be, but you know, it's your database so let's respect it by making sure everybody's happy with it."

Step 4: What (Do You Want To Say To The Host Business' Customers)?

It's important your strategy has a clear focus, and you know precisely what you're setting out to achieve.

The first thing to think about is whether the letter to customers will be from you or your host business.

Generally, the most successful host beneficiary letters come from the host business. For example, the letter, which would could come from a beauty salon, goes something like this: "Hi there, I know a great hairdresser called Harry. As a special gift from me, I've arranged for you to have your hair styled by Harry for nothing. Call 1236 8855 to make your appointment. Tell Harry I sent you."

This type of letter tends to work well. The customers believe the business owner has gone out of the way to organise a special deal for them. They tend to feel obligated to take it up.

If you were to write to the beauty salon's customers, saying, "Hi, my name's Harry I cut hair, and I've been doing it for 12 years," it's unlikely people will call. There is nothing special about the offer. In fact, there's no offer at all. You're just like any other hairdresser making a claim about how good you are and how much experience you have. It's much better when someone else is tooting your horn for you.

Once you decide which way to go, you then have to write the letter. You see, even if you decide the letter will come from the host business, it's still up to you to write it. They just sign it and put their name to it.

Your letter needs to have a clear purpose, and take people from point A to point B. Point A is your headline, which should identify where they are now. The body of the letter leads them to Point B, which is where you tell them why they should act right now, and how to do it.

Most important is understanding the customers you're writing to. If you understand their needs, wants and current position, you can sell almost anything to them. For instance, mailing a letter to 47-year-old women with a headline that says, "Concerned about menopause? Here's why you don't need to be," could yield excellent results. Or what about a letter to 17-year-olds that says, "Forget the fake ID ... here's how you can get access to Sydney's best nightclubs before your 18th." Or how about a letter to struggling musicians that says, "Tired of people passing your talent by? Here's how to take the bull by the horns and get famous ... within 14 months."

These letters reach out and speak to the people reading them. If you don't understand whom you're writing to, you'll inevitably get off on the wrong foot with them. Before writing anything, you need to decide exactly what message you want to communicate. Then you need to decide what you want the recipients of your letter to do about it.

The first example (the beauty salon who gives the customers a free haircut) is an excellent one. It has a clear purpose. The flow from Point A to Point B is clear. Here's a more detailed explanation:

Point A:	The customer knows of the business, and has dealt with them a few times before. They've been happy with the service and trust the business owner.
Body Copy:	You know me; I think you're a special customer. I wanted to say thanks, so here's a gift – a free haircut. I highly recommend Harry, he's great and here's why. Call him soon. I too look forward to hearing from you soon.
Point B:	The customer calls and makes an appointment for a free haircut.

It pays to remember that simply asking people to act now is rarely enough. You need to give them a good reason why they should do something. A letter that just has a recommendation from the host business is OK, but a killer offer that is limited in some way will work ten times better.

Remember, most purchases can be delayed forever. It's one thing to create desire, but it's another to actually get people to part with their cash.

The next question you have to answer is, how do you offer a great deal without slicing your profit margin drastically? There's a couple of ways. First, make sure you are selling products or services with a high margin. Often, that's not possible, but if you have the option of gearing your business towards higher margin items, do so as it's then much easier to come up with great deals.

If you can't, you need to find items or services that are highly valued by your customers, yet have low costs. You could even be super-tricky and arrange a host beneficiary for your host beneficiary.

Here's how this works: You offer the customers of the host business something extra if they come and buy from you. You get this something extra free from another business. You are now also a host business. For example, the hairdresser could write to the customers of the beauty salon and offer a free bottle of Mathew James Shampoo with any haircut. Matthew James, wanting to convert customers to their brand, would offer the shampoo for free.

You'll find more details on offers in Part 10.

Step 5: How (Do You Write Your Letter)?

Once again, I want to dispel a common misconception. You don't have to be a wizard with words to write a letter that works. Anyone can. You just need to know the people you're writing to and know how to come up with a good offer.

Simply going to a database of stressed-out executives and saying, "100% less stress in 10 minutes or it's free ... guaranteed. Normally $15. We come to you. Phone 4563 4525 for a FREE introductory session," is enough. It doesn't matter what language you use, or even if you make spelling mistakes. Now I know you may find this strange, but believe me, most people won't even know.

As long as your message is clear, quick and targeted well, your letter will work. Once again, I'm going to stress the one thing you MUSN'T do, and that's getting off the point, or rambling on too long. If every word and every sentence says something important, fine. If your letter is full of guff, people will lose interest very quickly. These guidelines also apply to any letters you may write to the host business, when floating the idea or arranging the relationship, or letters you write to their customers.

Here are some other guidelines for getting your letter just right.

Your Headline

Tell people exactly what they'll get from reading the letter. The headline lets prospects know whether they should bother reading on. It needs to promise immediate benefits. For example, 'Here's how to make $4500 extra income this month (just by sleeping in two hours later)' or 'Save 56% on your insurance bill.'

The other approach is to invoke curiosity. This is harder to do effectively, but better if your product doesn't contain a striking benefit. Here's a good example. 'Here's why 3 out of 4 Auckland children will lose their hair before they reach 17' or '4 reasons to call George's Gym before July 15 and say "I'm a willee-wrinkle-wowee"'.

Most importantly, your headline needs to stop readers dead in their tracks. Another trick is to speak directly to them in your headline. For example, why not make your headline something like this: 'George, here's how you can make an extra $19,000 this year and make Harriet happy.' If you have your customer's first names, it's easy to do with computer software.

Create A Strong Introduction

The first couple of sentences are incredibly important. They tell people whether they should read on in depth or start skimming. Nine out of ten times they'll skim (or trash the letter entirely).

Here are a couple of powerful introductions that help get higher readership levels:

'Before you start skimming, just stop. Stop and think about where your life is heading.' Or, 'You don't know it yet, but the next five paragraphs contain the secrets of earning a fortune, without breaking your back.'

You need to immediately let people know they're doing the right thing by reading. Here's another 'cut them off at the pass' style introduction:

'I know you're tempted to throw this letter away without reading it, but I have a warning for you.'

Of course, in most cases your first paragraph will just support your headline. For example, 'You're probably a little disbelieving. In fact, I'm certain you think I'm pulling your leg, but let me show you why this headline is 100% true.'

Generally, with a host beneficiary letter, the introduction should refer to the relationship between the host and the customer. For example, 'I wanted to write and say thanks,' or even, 'it's so rare that anyone says thank you.'

Include A Strong, Specific Call To Action

Here's another golden rule to remember: If you don't tell people what to do, they probably won't do anything. Give them precise instructions on what to do; who to call, which number to use, when to do it and what to ask for. Here's a good example: 'Call Gordon Harris now on 3345 6756 and ask for your 45 page personal astrological analysis chart.'

Better still, tell them to act and then mention you'll be phoning in the next couple of days to further discuss the letter and offer. Naturally, it depends if the host business is willing to give you phone numbers. I must say, they rarely do.

Include Concise And Convincing Body Copy

The body copy is the actual text between the introduction and the call to action. Once again, you don't need to be a great writer to do this part well. It's far more important you get your point across clearly, in as few words as possible, and in a logical order.

Editing is another vitally important task. Every word must count, so after you've written your first draft, go through it with a fine-tooth comb and edit viciously. Next, read it aloud to make sure it flows. Lastly, have a couple of people check it through and ask what they understood from it. This is to make sure you're getting your point across. Ask which parts were boring and don't be afraid of the criticism. You didn't set out to be the world's greatest writer anyway, so any comments should be helpful, rather than hurtful.

Sub-Headlines

If your letter is a long one (and by that I mean anything over two pages), it's important to break up your text with sub-headlines.

These are short mini-headlines that guide the reader through the letter and pique their interest. There's nothing wrong with making each one as attractive as your main headline.

Use A PS

One of the most important aspects of the copy is the PS. In fact, the PS is often the most read part of the letter. It pays to include a major point right at the end. For example, an extra special bonus if the offer is taken up within the next three days.

People tend to read the PS because it's unexpected. They are often surprised someone has forgotten to include something. Some professional copywriters use up four PS's and write up to half a page for each.

Make The Layout 'Fun'

When writing your letter, forget everything you learnt at school about writing a so-called business letter.

Indent paragraphs, splash bold throughout, use bullet points and give everything lots of space. If you look at your letter and think, 'My god, that's a lot,' you need to take another look at your layout. Perhaps it needs to be spread out. Or maybe you need to put the main points of a paragraph in bullet point form.

Watch Out For Letters That Are Too Long Or Too Short

The number of pages is less important than the actual layout. If spacing it out spills the letter over onto three pages rather than one, that's fine just as long as it looks 'fun' to read.

Host Beneficiary Relationships

Here's another common misconception I want to dispel: A one-page letter will always be read. Now there may be some truth to that, but there's also a lot of mistruth mixed in there too. If the letter is packed solid with text just so it'll fit on one page, people will be more turned off than if it were four pages and well spaced.

Likewise, if it's not interesting and un-targeted, people won't read it out of politeness. And if it doesn't have enough meat and reasons to act, people won't do anything. You need to say enough to get them inspired to do something, but not so much that they run out of time, or get bored.

For a host beneficiary letter, it's unlikely you'll need anything more than two pages. If you do, it's either a special case, or you're waffling. The personal recommendation from the business owner should be enough of a selling point to get you over most objections.

Avoid Anything That's Hard To Read

Type your letter in a standard font: Times New Roman or Courier. Always bear in mind that whilst an elaborate font may look nicer, it'll be harder to read. Remember, people aren't interested in playing games by trying to decipher your bizarre typeface; they just want to know if they should bother reading and if they like what they read, what they should do.

Don't make things confusing, as it'll only obscure your message. I always say avoid being an artist; be a business person instead.

Include A Gimmick

The very best direct mail letters contain some sort of gimmick. Something out of the ordinary that makes them memorable and interesting.

Here are a few examples:

A letter headed, 'Here's why life is sweeter when you're with MGA Insurance,' included a lollipop.

A piece of salami was sent with a letter. The tie-in was that one rotten piece could bring down a whole company. At the time, the 'salami incident' (where a piece of salami allegedly poisoned and killed a young girl, subsequently destroying the company) was still fresh in the minds of the readers. The letter was for an employment agency, which helped you weed out the 'rotten apples.'

40 cents was taped to the top of a letter. The headline was, 'I'm so eager to show you the new range of Grubic Motorcycles, I've already paid for you to phone me.'

A small bag of fertiliser was mailed with a letter to agricultural wholesalers. The headline was, 'Here's 30g of Australia's most advanced fertiliser. Here's why you'll soon need 30 tonnes of the stuff.'

A gimmick is a brilliant way to get attention, and to stop people in their tracks. It's also great if you're following your letter up with a phone call. Imagine calling after mailing the letter with the piece of salami. Instead of the usual, 'Oh, I don't know. I may have read it,' reply, you'd get, 'Oh, that letter!'

Whether you can do this will heavily depend on the business owner and how far they're willing to go.

Try and follow up the letter with a phone call. Most people won't call straight off your letter anyway. That's just the nature of the game. However, if you mail them a letter, then call soon after, you'll be surprised by the leap in response you'll experience. That's because people will have the chance to ask you questions, and then to order directly.

A Special Note About Approaching Host Businesses

The main thing to bear in mind is you're doing the host business a favour. If they truly understand what you're proposing, they should jump at the chance.

Here's the simplest explanation: you're going to give them something worth $x they can give to their customers for free. Perhaps it's a free voucher, or an information booklet.

When their customers receive the gift, they'll think highly of the business owner and be appreciative. They'll probably become more loyal and give more referrals.

Imagine if a business sent you a free gift every month. One month it would be a haircut, the next a voucher for having your lawn mowed, then an opportunity to get massaged for free.

You'd feel pretty happy about this, wouldn't you? You'd probably feel privileged to be a part of this business, and there's a very high chance you'd want to do business with them again.

If you, as a business owner, can see the benefit in this, then remember that when you approach the host businesses. If you want to start sending your own customers gifts, you have to go out and find someone who will offer a free gift. It's harder than you think.

You're making it easy; you're fronting up with a free gift the host businesses can present to its customers. You're the one putting yourself out. There are certain concessions you may need to make to ensure the deal happens. Here are a list of things you can offer the host business if there's any doubt:

- **You pay for the postage:** If they don't ask you to pay for the postage, then all well and good. You're getting off lightly. Remember, it's your idea, so you should pay for it. The best you're likely to get is half and half. The host may offer to drop it in with a mailing they're already doing, but you'd be better off paying for a separate mailing.
- **You pack the envelopes:** There's no reason why you should ask the business owner to do anything aside from providing the names. They may want to stick labels on so you don't get to keep the names.
- **You agree you will only use the names once:** If they give you their list, you should probably guarantee that once this promotion's over, you won't touch the names again.
- **You will do the same thing for them later down the track:** If you're not willing to do the same for them, why should they do it for you?

Step 6: When (To Mail Your Letters)

If your product is perennial you don't have to be too concerned about when to implement your strategy. It's more a question of which day, rather than which time of year.

With business clients, it's usually a good idea to mail them a letter on Tuesday or Wednesday. People are usually feeling too busy on Monday and pretty uninterested in thinking about anything new on Friday. On course, if your business is seasonal, you need to approach it differently.

Step 7: What Else (Do You Need To Think About)?

Use this section as a final checklist. Once you're happy with your strategy letter, run through and make sure you're ready to get started. Here are a few things you may not have thought of.

Team Training

Does your team fully understand the strategy you've implemented? It's important they understand the vital role they are to play in it. If your new customers come in and find anything less than the highest level of service, your campaign will fail.

Objects

Have you included an item with each letter? Check and make sure all letters contain the object you've mentioned in the opening paragraph. Your letter will not make much sense without it.

Check Stock and Team Levels

It's unlikely your campaign will bring in hundreds of people all at once, but you need to be prepared just in case. There would be nothing worse than having a rush of new customers come in only to find you have no stock or are too busy to serve them.

"So what do you think, Charlie?"

"This is awesome stuff, Brad. I see what you mean. If I choose my host beneficiaries correctly, they'll be helping me get new leads and I'll be helping them in return by giving them something of value to give to their own customers. Sounds like a win-win situation to me."

"That's absolutely right. Establish a working relationship with the right business and it can generate so much business for you, you'll wonder how you ever managed without it. And the real winner here, apart from you, has got to be the customer. Think about it – isn't that what good business is all about?"

"You're making sense, Brad. Now, who do you think I should approach?"

"You have many options. But remember, they must be allied but non-competitive businesses. That way you not only add value to what ever it is your host beneficiary company does, but you'll be generating leads from a pool of customers who are already pre-qualified. By that, I mean they are already interested in what you can offer. You see, if you were for instance, to set up a host beneficiary arrangement with the local baker, it would probably bring in new customers, but how many of the baker's customer base would have no interest in what it is you do?"

"What do you mean?"

"Think of it this way – do you need to own a car to be a regular customer of a bakery? No. You could be a retired pensioner who doesn't drive, a schoolgirl who hasn't got her drivers licence yet or anyone else who doesn't own a car. Sure, some will, but it's not a pre-requisite. So tapping into that customer list won't be as effective, or lucrative, from your point-of-view as appealing to customers of a business that only deals with motorists. Get it?"

"Sure do, Brad. So I should be thinking about panel beaters, car yards and windscreen repairers."

"That's right, Charlie. But there's more. You should also think about approaching caravan sales businesses, boat yards, tow bar fitment centers or auto accessories stores. There's quite a few, when you really begin to think about it."

Charlie's mind was racing. He picked up his pencil and began scribbling notes on his pad. He was on a roll, so I got up and strolled across to the workshop entrance, eager to leave him to it. I also wanted to see what cars were in – just a little passion of mine, you know.

After a leisurely stroll between the work bays and an exchange of pleasantries with the blokes, I returned to the office to find Charlie all smiles, sitting back and waiting for me.

"I think you'll like this one, mate," he said as he slid a sheet of paper across to me. I read it carefully, then said, "This is great, Charlie. I'm real proud of you. You've done well."

This is what he came up with:

Here's how you can give each of your customers a surprise gift ...

... and it won't cost you a cent

Dear Jimmy,

You're probably wondering what this is all about, so I'll tell you straight away - I'm about to give you an easy way to delight your customers.

Best of all, I'm going to pay for it. Let me explain...

I want you to send every one of your customers a gift – the opportunity to take advantage an EXCLUSIVE, once-off deal. Here's the offer – 2 major services for less than the price of 1.

If your customers visit Charlie's Garage, we'll treat their cars to a full service like they've never experienced before at a price they won't believe. That's right – I want to give each of your customers **$169 worth of workshop services for just $75.**

You're probably wondering how this will benefit you.

Simple - the gift will come from your business, not from me. Each of your clients will think that this is a special deal that YOU have arranged for them. Best of all, this entire promotion won't cost you a cent. All you need to do is mail them the letter I've included for you (I'll cover the cost of the printing and postage).

Actually, **I'll even prepare all the letters** - you just need to stick address labels on and send them out.

Just imagine how impressed your clients will be when they receive this unexpected gift. Better still, imagine how many of their friends they're going to tell. This is a sure-fire way to keep your current clients happy and get some referrals along the way.

I'll give you a call in the next couple of days to arrange the fine details.

Thanks, and I look forward to seeing you soon ...

Charlie
Charlie's Garage

PS Of course, I wouldn't want you to recommend us without visiting us first.
   Please accept my offer of a free major service.

2 Major services for less than the price of 1

Hi [NAME],

Firstly, I'd like to say thanks for dealing with Jimmy's Windscreens. Loyal customers like yourself really make doing business a pleasure.

As a token of my appreciation, I've arranged something special for you – a unique offer from Charlie's Garage, a mechanical workshop in Brisbane's western suburbs.

Here's the deal – visit Charlie's Garage, and you'll receive 2 major services for your car for the amazing price of just $75 each (plus parts). That would normally cost you $169 each.

We have arranged this special deal for our top customers as a surprise gift. Jimmy's Windscreens understands that good customers deserve awesome treatment and service, and I think it's important to say 'thanks' every once in a while, and to do something unexpected.

And just so you know that you'll be dealing with one of the best mechanical workshops, let me tell you 3 things about Charlie's Garage ...

1. **They're serious about results** ... Charlie's Garage is not your average garage. Using the latest equipment, they service a wide range of cars and have a large, loyal customer base.

2. **They're professional AND friendly** ... Charlie will personally deal with you before, during and after servicing your car. And he has a team of 4 highly qualified and experienced mechanics on his team.

3. **You'll be totally satisfied** ... when Charlie's Garage looks after your car, you'll be totally satisfied with the entire experience – guaranteed, or your money back.

I seriously recommend you take advantage of this special offer. I know that you'll appreciate the thought!! Simply phone Charlie and mention that you have this letter.

Once again, I'd like to say thank you for being a valued client of Jimmy's Windscreens, and I look forward to seeing you again soon,

Jimmy
Jimmy's Windscreens

PS There's only one limitation on this voucher - you need to use it **before 28 July 2002**. It's worth acting soon – this is the only time this century you will be able to get your car services twice for less than it would normally cost to do once.

PPS I've included a Charlie's Garage business card, with their contact details. **Phone for a personal appointment**, and make sure you take this letter when you drop in.

Examples

Here are some examples of letters that have been designed to get noticed, read and to attract more customers. The first is a letter a host business would mail to its database. The second is a letter a business would mail to a host business suggesting a campaign and the third is a letter that host business would mail to their customers.

These examples will give you a good idea of how the various letters should look. Keep in mind the information you've just learned and read over these examples carefully. It's a good idea to write out these examples, word for word, to become used to the style of writing that's required. Once you have a feel for it, have a go at writing your own.

Also, keep in mind when writing the letter to the host business that people won't sign anything that's over the top. Don't say anything about your company that people won't be happy to sign off on.

Example 1

Do You Have Any Expensive Jewellery You No Longer Wear?

Here's how to make every piece fashionable again.

Dear [name],

I've recently come across an excellent idea.

I'm not sure about you, but I've got lots of jewellery that I no longer wear. Either it doesn't fit my finger, or it's gone out of style. I mean, these rings still have immense sentimental value – they just aren't fashionable any more.

That's why re-making is such a great idea. Here's how it works:

You take your existing jewellery, extract the raw materials (gold, silver, gems) and create something completely new. Instead of purchasing a brand new piece, you modernise what you already have. The results can be truly startling, as the 'before and after' shots I've included illustrate.

Of course, you may be happy with the style; it could be the fit that's the problem. With re-sizing, it's easily taken care of. For less than you'd think, your ring can be re-shaped to fit your finger perfectly.

And best of all, I've arranged a free assessment for you. This is a 15-minute analysis with one of Auckland's finest jewellers – Brian Davis of Jolissa's Jewellers.

Mention you're a customer of Lejose and Brian will clean and polish your ring free. Then, after careful examination, he will explain the possibilities. You'll be amazed – the most archaic looking piece can be turned into something sophisticated and dazzling.

This assessment comes with no obligation. It's simply an opportunity to see how easily your old, unused jewellery can be transformed.

Phone Brian now on 478 3112, or simply drop in.

Julie McNamara

Lejose

PS If you have your ring remade in the next 28 days, you'll receive a special bonus - a $50 voucher to spend at Lejose.

Example 2

Good morning NAME ...

Here's a $195.00 gift you can give every one of your customers ... FREE

I've come up with a great idea.

A way that we, as business people who both deal with homeowners, can help each other.

It won't cost you anything; it'll fit in with your current promotional efforts and it's guaranteed to make your current customers feel special. More importantly, it'll give them another good reason to come back and buy from you again (or recommend that their friends do).

Here's the idea ...

I manage a company called The Mortgage Professionals – we help people slash their mortgage. And when I say slash, I mean that literally – one guy I recently dealt with saved 12 years and $37,000.

Whilst that's exceptional, it's not rare ... this happens all the time. We are NOT a bank, or financial institution – just intermediaries.

More on that later. First, I want to explain how this applies to you ...

People usually pay $195 for us to go over their numbers and work out a plan. This is a 30-minute session, and the first step in the process. I've recently had 500 x $195 vouchers printed – these cover the cost of this initial consultation. Of course, there's no obligation to go ahead with anything, but it will give the person an idea of what's possible.

Here's where you come in ...

I'm happy for you to distribute these vouchers to your customers. They're genuinely valued at $195.00 each; it'd make an excellent gift for your customers.

I've also written a letter, which I'd like you to send out with the vouchers. Even better than that, I'm willing to pay for the postage, printing and envelopes – all you need to do is stick on the address labels. I won't see the list, and won't have the opportunity to contact your customers unless they contact me.

It's a fantastic way to do something special for your customers without really doing very much at all. All you need to do is say "yes" when I call and I'll organise for everything to go ahead.

And remember – this promotion won't cost you anything, and is a brilliant, meaningful way to treat your past customers.

I'll call you in the next few days, just to answer any questions you have, and organise the finer details ...

Look forward to speaking with you then,

Shane Holzheimer

The Mortgage Professionals.

PS   If you're looking for an explanation of how this works, you'll find it in the small booklet I've included with this letter. I'll answer any extra questions you have when I call.

PPS For each person who goes ahead with a mortgage plan, we'll post you a 5% 'spotters fee' – that's around $130.

PPPS This idea comes with the full backing of Citibank.

Example 3

YOU Can Slash Up To 8 Years And $65,000 Off Your Mortgage
(Without Increasing Repayments.)

Good morning,

I recently discovered something exciting – a way you can literally slash your mortgage by thousands, and own your home sooner.

This has nothing to do with banks, or swapping your loan over. It's through a company called The Mortgage Professionals.

Here's a basic explanation of how it works ...

* Your full income is paid directly into your loan ...

* You pay your monthly expenses using a 55 days interest-free credit card ...

* An automatic sweeper account pays off your credit card at the end of the month, meaning you pay no interest ...

This is backed by Citibank, and has already worked for dozens of Brisbane residents. Some people have saved over $60,000 in repayments, and will now own their home almost a decade sooner.

All without increasing their repayments!!

The first step is a 30-minute appointment with a Mortgage Professionals consultant. This costs $195. Or at least, it usually costs $195. I've arranged for you to have your consultation FREE. That's right – as a valued customer of [business name], I've already covered this fee for you.

I highly recommend it, and expect you'll reap massive benefits from the idea. Hope you enjoy my gift – may it be the start of something great ...

Part 5

▌Strategic Alliances

"What we're now going to work on is a strategy that's similar to host beneficiaries, Charlie. It's called a Strategic Alliance."

"Excellent, Brad. I'm really beginning to enjoy myself."

"I've always maintained business should be fun, Charlie. And it always amazes me how many business people seem to hate what they do. They seem to think getting up in the morning to go to work is the hardest thing in the world. It really shouldn't be. You see, if we spend most of our lives at work, we might as well enjoy it, don't you think?"

"I couldn't agree more, Brad. You know how much I love cars. I could spend all day working on them. But I must admit, I always did think of the paperwork involved as being a bit of a drag. In fact, I used to put it off until I just had to attend to it. But now I'll view it very differently."

"I'm glad to hear it, Charlie. You see, it's what you do in the office that's going to make all the difference to your business. You can always hire great mechanics, but if you don't get the work in for them, they'll leave. Or more likely, you'll have to ask them to leave because you won't be able to pay them."

He sat there, nodding at every word I said. Charlie was a smart man, and a good worker. That was half his problem, from a business point-of-view, of course. I had long seen how he relished the opportunity of poking his head under my car's bonnet. He couldn't help himself, really. Tinkering with cars was his thing – it always had been.

And he isn't alone. Most small business owners are in exactly the same boat. You see, they start up their own business or buy one that they feel comfortable with. By this I mean they get involved in an area of their expertise. It's only natural, I suppose, but from a business point-of-view, it doesn't make good sense. They end up working IN the business and not ON it.

Charlie was beginning to realise this.

"A strategic alliance is when you and another business enter into a loose partnership to help each other make extra profits. For example, a tree lopper may refer work to a lawn mower, and vice versa. They may give each other 10% of the price tag of any referred work. Suddenly, each has a 'scout' working for them."

He was listening intently.

"The number of suppliers the tree lopper may do this with is unlimited, although it's probably wise to work with only one of each type of business."

What Is A Successful Strategic Alliance?

The answer to this question is simple – if you make more money from the strategic alliance than it cost you, it's been a success. Of course, you need to put a value on your time also. If it costs you no money but takes three days a week, that needs to be taken into account also.

Ultimately, any strategic alliance campaign that pays for itself can be considered successful. Before getting started, there are a few things you need to think about in depth:

Work Out Your Costs

This includes the cost of printing, envelopes, phone calls, liaising with the other business owners, and more.

Know Your Margins

You need to know the net profit you make from anyone who buys your product or service. By understanding how much you actually make from each sale, you'll be able to work out the percentage response required to make your campaign profitable. Factor in everything; right down to the pencils you use to write out quotes. At the end of the day, many businesses fail, because they don't count the little things. What looks like a great profit margin is quickly whittled down to nothing by items such as petrol, stationery, and business lunches. The more accurate you can be, the better the decisions you'll make.

Lifetime Value

You will normally lose money on the first sale you make to a new client, so don't view them as a once-off sale. Any strategic alliance campaign that covers its cost initially will turn out to be very profitable in the long-term. If you simply cover your costs in the short-term, you'll have a successful strategy on your hands.

In many cases, you should consider the strategic alliance an exercise in 'buying' customers. This means you are giving away money in exchange for a new customer. Remember, a new and loyal customer will make you a healthy income over the course of your lifetime.

What Makes A Successful Strategic Alliance?

I'm now only going to give you a broad overview of what makes a strategic alliance successful. More specific and in depth details will be discussed shortly.

For a start, I want to mention a few key elements that are crucial to the success of any strategic alliance campaign.

The Right Attitude

Never forget you're doing the other business a favour as well. You need to understand they're getting as much benefit as you are. When you approach them, do so from a position of power. Your attitude should be: "I'm going to help you out. This is a great opportunity, but I'm going to be selective." Of course, if your offer to the other businesses is not strong, you'll be fighting an uphill battle from the outset.

Targeted Lists

You don't want to deal with businesses and customers that are unrelated to your line of work. You need to choose businesses that deal with almost identical customers to those you do. For example, people who own expensive cars, people who are absolute music fanatics, or ladies over 30 with acne problems. Your customers need to be definable in terms of age, sex, interests or income.

Offer

A strong offer will make all the difference. Without one, you can forget about achieving a response. With a powerful offer, you may need to hire extra team members just to cope with the response. This relates to the offer you are making the other businesses, and the offer you are making their customers to come and deal with you.

Support From The Other Business

If your ally business gets right behind the idea, you'll have a far better chance of success. If not, you're fighting an uphill battle. You need to get them on board right from the start and you need to make sure they approach the project with a 'this is gonna be great' attitude.

Follow-Up

Once you've set up the alliance, you need to maintain it. Keep regular contact with the ally business, and keep giving them reasons to help you out. Obviously, if you're working hard for them, they'll work hard for you.

Don't expect it to be all your own way – there has to be give and take. Of course, this is a small price to pay for a strong alliance, as you're gaining a new source of customers, which will undoubtedly cost you less than advertising, direct mail, flyers or Yellow Pages would. Better yet, the customers come 'referred', which means they come with a good attitude. They will look for the good things about your service, and be less suspicious. They're also unlikely to go shopping for better deals. They've heard good things about you, which means they want to give you every opportunity to please them. And as you'd be aware, these customers are pretty rare. It's worth working hard to develop an alliance that provides you with a steady stream of them.

The 6 Steps To Creating Strategic Alliances

Step 1: Why (Use A Strategic Alliance)?

Before doing anything, you need to work out whether a strategic alliance is for you.

You need to compare its potential returns against other strategies for marketing yourself.

For example, if your market is broad and your offer is VERY appealing, why not use the newspaper instead? It's easier and probably a cheaper too. Or what about radio? These methods will give you immediate access to a large market and you don't have to worry about setting up a middleman. Of course, this will only work if your business has broad appeal, and a point of uniqueness (a great deal, exclusive products, or an amazing service).

A strategic alliance is ideal when you have a specific group of people you want to advertise to and there are other non-competitive businesses already dealing with them.

Remember our previous example about the corporate training organizations? They know who their target market is (businesses that need help with customer service and sales), and the businesses that already deal with them (firms like stationery suppliers and computer shops).

Remember, strategic alliances work best because the potential customer thinks the other business is doing them a favour by giving them a tip: "Deal with these guys and they'll really take care of you."

The customer believes the business has gone out of its way to make a recommendation, which will help them. Because of that, they feel some obligation to take action. You need to find businesses that are willing to get behind the idea 100%, or forget it altogether.

This brings us to the other consideration – are there any businesses out there who are willing to open their minds enough to run with the idea?

Of course, it depends how you bring it up with them. If you say, "Listen, I want to use you and then steal your customers," you'll have a bit of a battle getting their agreement. On the other hand, you could try an approach like this: "Hi there, I've got a way we can help each other. I'll get some new customers, and you'll get some new customers. We'll also start making an extra couple of hundreds bucks a week, pure profit." It's certain you'll get a better response from this method.

Step 2: Who (Is Your Target Market)?

Before you even start making a list of strategic allies, you need to identify exactly whom it is you're trying to reach. Precisely who is your target market? A failure to answer this question will lead to failure FOREVER. For example, imagine a company who sells in-ground swimming pools doing a mailing campaign to a block of high-rise rental apartments. You'd be a fool to bet on anything other than a dismal and costly blowout.

To avoid mistakes, you need to know exactly who your potential customers are before you start arranging alliances with anyone.

So let's get specific – who are the people most likely to be interested in your product or service? These are the kind of characteristics to identify:

Age: How old are they?

Sex: Are they male or female? The reality is, your business probably appeals more to the male psyche, or the female psyche.

Income: How much do they make? If your customers are quality driven, it may be time to re-assess those 'Half Price' ads. If you discover they want the cheapest thing they can find, you'd better start looking at the offers you're making.

Where do they live: Are they local, or do they come from miles around to deal with you? This will dictate how you communicate with them. If your customers are local and it's unlikely they'd travel more than 10km to deal with you, you should search for a strategic ally that is based close to where you are. People generally do not drive all the way across town to get their hair cut, at least not on a regular basis.

Step 3: Which (Business Will Make A Good Ally)?

Now you've identified the 'who' you need to find the right business to help you reach them.

Strategic Alliances

There are a number of criteria for selecting an ally business. If you can think of one that matches all of these points, you can feel secure in selecting them as an ally. If you can find a few that meet most of the criteria, it will probably be still worth running the strategy. Here's your checklist:

Non-Competitive

This means they don't sell what you sell, or anything that could be considered a replacement for what you sell. An ideal example of non-competitive businesses would be a carpet dealer and a lighting store. The major market for both is people moving into new homes. The fact is, people can't choose to buy lighting OR floor coverings; they must buy both. Therefore, both businesses are in an excellent position to help each other. The carpet dealer could agree to give out gift vouchers on behalf of the lighting store. The lighting store could do the same for the carpet dealer. Immediately, both would get new business.

Each would tap into the customers the other business is attracting. These customers should be almost identical.

Of course, if you manage to get a semi-competitive business to promote you, then more power to you. It's their loss, not yours. Usually, there's a lot of grey area here as all businesses are competitive in one way or another. Everybody wants the same type of customer ... one with money to spend.

Some business owners are too paranoid to bother with. They think you're going to steal their customers. There's not much you can do about people like this. Just go for the ones with a good attitude.

Positioning

Of course, you do need to give consideration to the 'positioning' of the ally businesses. Here's what this means: the businesses creating the strategic alliance need to be at the same end of the quality and price spectrums. For example, if you deal only with sophisticated and wealthy customers, and your prices would send most middle income earners into panic, there's no point in creating an alliance with 'Crazy Bill's World of Discount Heart Transplants' or 'Cheap & A Little Bit Nasty.' Choose a business that shares a similar ethic to you.

Same Target Market

This is the most important consideration. The ally business must have the same, or a very similar, target market to yours.

For example, a high-class beauty salon and an exclusive hairdresser are very compatible, a Ford dealership and an auto-electrician specialising in Fords click well, as do a Hi-Fi shop and a CD store.

Think about what businesses YOU deal with yourself. Chances are, your customers have similar interests to you. Best of all, if you are already a loyal customer with one business, it should be easy to set up an alliance. For example, if you are a beautician and you've been going to the same hairdresser for years, it shouldn't be too difficult to say, "Why don't we help each other out?"

They Have A Database

Of course, it's not entirely essential. You can always ask the ally business to simply hand vouchers out, or make a verbal recommendation to their customers.

If they have a database, it means you can introduce yourself by letter. Better yet, get the owner of the business to write a letter recommending you.

Right Attitude

Be aware that many business owners are very cynical people who think the world owes them a living. Stay well clear of them. It's better to find someone who's willing to give you the support that you need. There are people out there like that, and they'll love to get involved.

Their Customers Like Them And They Like Their Customers

There are two things you don't want. The first is an ally business with customers that hate them and the second is to get a whole bunch of new customers who the ally business owner hates. You need to check that the ally business thinks highly of their customers.

Large Number Of Customers

If the ally business has only dealt with a very small number of customers, why would you bother, unless you were in the type of market that only has a handful of customers? Yes, they do exist.

If they have a huge number of customers, you may even want to offer exclusivity to the business in exchange for access to the whole customer base, including phone numbers.

Of course, the more successful businesses will be harder to convince. They don't need the customers that you will send them, especially if you are smaller than they are.

You need to ask this question when considering an ally business: "They've got so much to offer me. Do I have anything to offer THEM?" If you don't, you may have to think again. It's probably worth a try, but you may have to be a little less ambitious.

A Willingness To Test

It's important you stress to the ally business that you just want to do everything on a small scale before a large one. If the business owner says no, it's a less than ideal situation. Thank the business owner, but stress it's best to test first.

You could say to the ally business owner, "I think we should do a hundred first, just to make sure that everything's OK. I mean, of course it will be, but you know, it's your customer base so let's respect it and just make sure everybody's happy with it."

And of course, you want to keep reminding the business owner of the ultimate outcome. Make it clear everything may not work perfectly at first, but it's worth spending the time refining the idea.

Step 4: What (Can You Offer The Ally Business)?

Remember, this is business ... not something based on friendship. You need to work out precisely how much you can offer these businesses. You need to work out what you'll sacrifice in order to make this arrangement work. Here are some ideas:

Commission

This is the old stand-by. This tends to work well in any situation. There are very few people who would turn down extra money in their pockets. If you are going to sell the idea on this basis, give the potential ally business owner an idea of how much they will be making each week.

If you say, "I'll give you 10% of every job you send me," people don't tend to get very excited. 10% doesn't sound like much. Why not phrase it this way: "You deal with about 50 customers a week, don't you? If you refer one in every ten, that's five customers a week. My average sale is $500 per customer. That adds up to $250 extra profit in your pocket each week. And all you have to do is give them this voucher and say a couple of good words about me."

Big difference?

Why not be a bit more generous when thinking about how much to offer. Consider the lifetime value of the customer. You'd be better off just covering your costs and banking on the customer coming back to you.

Of course, it depends on your business. A hairdresser can rely on lifetime value whereas a car salesman can't. If you do expect to see the customer back, why not give the ally business all the profit from the first sale. It'll certainly boost the number of customers they send you.

You Send Customers To Them

If you are in a position to send them customers, offer it first. Why give away any profit if you can get away with a quid pro quo arrangement instead? Although it will mean you'll need to change your sales process, it beats writing big cheques to the ally business.

There are a couple of challenges with doing it that way. The first is, how much are you doing for them in relation to how much are they doing for you? You may find you keep sending them customers, but they never send you a thing.

The other challenge may result if you rarely send them a new customer. Your follow-up will be awkward. How can you encourage them to do anything for you, if you haven't done anything for them? They'll tell you to get lost.

Only go down this path if you're certain you can give the other business a good deal. If you are already sending your customers to this type of business, chances are this system will work well for you.

Benefits Appeal

This is the most risky and the hardest way to set up your strategic alliance. Even so, it's the most satisfying.

Explained simply, this is where you give the ally business good reasons to send their customers to you. For example, you may have the best product for the best price, or something completely unique that sets you apart from your competitors.

The only thing you offer to the ally business is the security of knowing they are sending their customers to the best business possible. This system works well if the ally business HAS to refer their clients somewhere. For example, an optometrist has to give people an idea of where to buy glasses.

All you need to do is write potential ally businesses a letter explaining what makes you different. If all you have to offer is good service and competitive prices, forget it. You need a uniqueness that makes them sit up and take notice of you – something that gets them talking.

There's nothing wrong with wining and dining them. People like to help people they know and like. If you develop a relationship with the ally, you're more likely to get the business.

Step 5: How (Do Set Up Your Strategic Alliance)?

There are many ways to set up a strategic alliance and many variations of the main types. I'm going to discuss the basics here, but please think laterally; combine or mix and match the various elements to suit your own situation.

Set Up A Referral System

This is where you get together with one or two other businesses and offer them reasons to refer customers to you.

As mentioned previously, the reasons can be commission, extra customers or just the knowledge they'll be referring their customers to a quality business.

The most effective type of referral system is a combination of all three. That is, you have a system where you give 10% of any referred job back to the referring business. They do the same for you. In addition, you ensure you give them plenty of supporting reasons – your service, your prices, and your quality.

Simply find a number of businesses that you feel would make good referees, and write them letters explaining the system. You'll find an example at the end of this section. Better yet, phone the businesses that have already been referring customers to you. Thank them directly for all their help and send them a gift. After that, say, "Listen, if you're doing this anyway, it's only fair I give some of the extra profits you're creating for me."

Not only will they jump at the idea, you'll find you immediately get more referrals, especially when you offer to start repaying the favour.

It's important to keep the relationship going after the initial contact and to build ongoing rapport. And remember, the more referrals you send them, the more they are likely to send you.

Choose your businesses well, as those with the wrong attitude and target market will only end up wasting your time. Re-read the guidelines already mentioned for choosing businesses.

Introduce yourself to the database of another business. This is the easiest way to join forces and something almost any business can do.

It's probably best explained with an example.

Let's imagine you run a small hairdressing business. You have a slew of regulars, but rarely see any new business owing to your poor location and dull advertising.

A pretty gloomy outlook? No problem! For less than the cost of one ad, you can have 300 customers personally recommended to you.

Here's how it works.

You arrange to meet with the owner of a non-competitive, yet related business. For a hairdresser, a beauty salon would be ideal. Dependent on the hairdresser's target market, a ladies gym might also be a winner.

Tell the business owner you are willing to give every one of their customers a free haircut, valued at $18.95. The trick is this: you're going to set it up so it looks as though the owner of the beauty salon has personally paid for this gift.

You write a letter, which is to be signed by the other business owner, that says, ' Thanks for being a customer – I appreciate it immensely. Just to show I truly am grateful, I've arranged a special gift for you ... a complimentary stylecut with Julia's Hairdressing. I recommend Julia and her team highly – and I'm certain you'll appreciate the difference too.'

You mail this letter to the beauty salon's entire database. To sweeten the deal, you might offer to pay for the postage and printing.

The benefit to the beauty salon is clear – they get to mail their customers an $18 gift without paying a cent for it. They get all the good feelings, referrals and repeat business and they didn't have to do a thing.

But the real benefits are yours. Hundreds of qualified people will receive a personal recommendation to see you for a haircut. They'll also get an almost irresistible offer.

Compare this with trying to get leads the traditional way – by placing an advertisement in the local newspaper. You spend $400; get 10 calls, and maybe 5 sales. Cost per sale: $80. That's pretty steep.

With the joining forces concept, the stats are a lot more appealing. A mailout to 200 people might cost you $150 all up. Let's imagine you get a 10% response (a pretty conservative estimate) – that's 20 new qualified customers. Cost per sale: $7.50.

Mmmmm, now it's starting to make sense.

Join forces with four or five related businesses, and form a 'collective'. This idea applies especially to people in the service industry.

Here's A Great Example

Let's say you're an auto electrician. You're doing OK, but most of the work is going elsewhere. The main mechanics in town are referring work to other guys, and you're getting killed in Yellow Pages.

What can you do? It's a tough one, although everyone who has a car may one day need your service, you just never know when. The answer is to join forces. Get on the phone to a mechanic, a car detailer, a tyre retailer and a window tinter. Tell them of your brilliant idea. Say, "Let's join forces!!"

Here's How It Works

You'll advertise yourselves under the one name; let's say 'Guaranteed Car Services' but you'll probably need to be a bit more creative than that. You have one number (a Freecall number), one guarantee (either the customer's delighted or they get the job for half price) and one policy – everyone helps everyone else out.

If the mechanic, window tinter, car detailer or tyre seller becomes aware of a car that needs an auto electrician, you get the details. If you see a mechanical problem, you pass the customer on to the mechanic. If the car detailer overhears a customer talking about tinting, they are referred to the window tinter.

At the end of every job, you run the customer through a checklist. "OK, that's your electrical problem sorted out. Now, when was the last time you had the car serviced? Right, I could arrange a service for you. Here's a $25 voucher towards that – I know the mechanic, Paul, and he does a top-notch job. Oh, by the way, summer's coming – have you thought about tinting? No, you should. I've got this card here from John's Auto Tinting. He said if I gave it to any of my customers, he'd do two windows for free when you make a booking to have your whole car done. And in case you didn't know, both of those guys are covered by Guaranteed Car Services. If you're not delighted with the result, you get your money back."

You run through your checklist, until each business has been covered. Any 'hot' leads get passed on to the relevant business and they return the favour for you. It takes a bit of organisation, but it's certainly worth it.

Here are three more interesting combinations:

a) **Guaranteed Home Services** - a lawn mower, water blaster, painter, roof restorer and tree stump removalist.

b) **Guaranteed Beauty** - a beauty salon, hairdresser, masseuse, psychic and gym.

c) **Guaranteed Fashion** - a clothes store, shoe shop, hat store, tie store and image consultant.

Open your mind to the possibilities - who could YOU join forces with?

Arrange free gifts to give to your customers. This is a reverse idea – where you introduce another business to your customers. It's a great one for businesses where there's a long interval between purchases.

Let's Think About A Car Salesperson.

The hardest thing about selling cars is getting people to remember who you are next time. Because, they often go two or three years without buying a car (and in many cases, much longer), there's very little loyalty.

That problem is easily solved – just keep in regular contact. Mail your customers cards, letters and communication. Just keep the relationship going. But if you're going to mail them something, why not make it extra special?

Drop down to the local clothes stores and say, "You know, most of my customers are young trendy women – they'd love to know more about your store. If you give me a $20 gift voucher for every one of my customers, I'll write a personal recommendation that they come and visit you."

Once you've got that out of the way, visit your next target business – a massage therapist. This time say, "Most of my customers have the money to spend on a monthly massage, and if they were shown how good it really is, I'm certain they'd be more than willing to come back regularly. If you give me a voucher for every one my customers, I'll mail it directly to them, and recommend they see you every four weeks."

OK, that should take care of your customers for a few months. Imagine that – you buy a car from someone, then start getting all these great gifts in the mail. How would that make you feel?

You can arrange gifts from almost any other business – either in the form of a gift voucher, a free service, a trial product, a 2 for 1 coupon, a free consultation, an in-home design service. The possibilities are endless.

Best of all, you won't have to pay a cent for any of it. And because it's your initiative (and not the dealerships), you take the list of names with you when you leave for another yard.

People buy off people, so if you've built the relationship, you get the sales.

Join forces with the suppliers of businesses you'd like to sell to ... this is an extension on the first idea.

Let's say you're a management consultant – you specialise in helping managers reach a state of peak performance. Simply introducing yourself directly could work, but it's really only you saying, "Hey, I'm good."

People expect you to toot your own horn. It's when someone else toots it for you that they get excited.

Strategic Alliances

So How Do You Do That?

Easy – hit the suppliers of the businesses you'd like to deal with. For example, their stationery supplier. You say to them, "I'd like to give you a gift, which you can pass on to your top clients. It'll make them love you, and give them some genuine benefits. I'm a management consultant, and I charge $456 an hour. For your clients, I'll do a full 1-hour appraisal and performance evaluation free of charge. This will be your gift to them."

To understand why this idea will work, you first need to understand the plight of the poor old stationery supplier. They're aware almost anyone with better prices can come along and knock them off their perch. There's so little differentiation between service; price is often the only factor.

Doing something out of the ordinary for their customers will give them the edge. They've introduced emotion into a very bland, price-driven business.

The benefit to you is also massive – you get a personal recommendation from someone the prospect already knows and trusts. For something as intangible as management consultancy and personal performance coaching, that's essential.

Sell Someone Else's Product

This is probably the most straightforward joining forces concept of them all. The trick is to be constantly scanning for hot products related to your business.

Getting back to our hairdresser, there are plenty of opportunities – a new quick-setting hairspray you spray just once, a hair dryer that runs on solar power yet generates more hot air than any on the market, a new hair colour that changes with the weather. You simply write your customers a letter explaining the benefits of the new product and end with, "Of course, I've arranged a special price for you. To order, simply call me now with your credit card details. I'll arrange postage within two days. And your purchase is guaranteed – If you're not delighted, simply phone me and I'll drop by and pick it up."

Suppliers generally won't mind, even if they're dealing direct with retail stores. It's another opportunity to sell the product after all.

You can also do this with service businesses. Simply take a commission on their first sale to the customer. For instance, a gym might sell a massage in a mail-out to the their customers. They do this on the condition they get half of the first sale. If the massage therapist is smart, she'll understand the lifetime value of the customer, and jump at the chance.

So, once you've decided which way to go with your strategic alliance strategy, you'll need to get out there and convince your potential ally businesses to get on board. The best way is to approach businesses that you already know, especially those that seem to be already referring customers to you.

Failing that, the best way is to write them a letter explaining the idea as clearly as you can, and then to follow-up with a phone call. And remember, you don't have to be a great writer to write a great letter. As long as your message is clear, quick and targeted well, your letter will work. Avoid the usual mistakes, like getting off the point, or rambling on. If every word and every sentence says something important, fine. But if you letter is full of mistakes, people will lose interest very quickly.

These guidelines apply for any letters you write to the ally business to arrange the relationship, or letters you write to their customers.

Here Are Some Other Guidelines For Getting Your Letter Just Right

Your Headline

Tell people exactly what they will get from reading the letter. The headline lets prospects know whether they should bother reading further. It needs to promise immediate benefits.

Create A Strong Introduction

The first couple of sentences are incredibly important. They tell people whether they should read on in-depth or start skimming. Generally, the introduction should refer to the relationship between the business and the customer. For example, "I wanted to write and say thanks," or even "It's so rare that anyone says thank you." Include a strong, specific call to action.

Include Concise And Convincing Body Copy

The body copy is the actual text between the introduction and the call to action. It's more important you get the point across clearly, in as few words as possible and in a logical order.

Sub-Headlines

If your letter is a long one (anything over two pages), it's important to break up your text with sub-headlines. These are short mini-headlines that guide the reader through the letter and pique their interest. There's nothing wrong with making each one as attractive as your main headline.

Use A PS

One of the most important aspects of the copy is the PS. In fact, the PS is often the most read part of the letter. It pays to include a major point right at the end – for example, an extra special bonus if the offer is taken up in the next three days.

Make The Layout 'Fun'

Indent paragraphs, splash bold throughout, use bullet points and give everything lots of space.

Watch Out For Letters That Are Too Long Or Too Short

The number of pages is less important than the actual layout. If spacing it out spills the letter over onto three pages rather than one, that's fine. Just as long as it looks fun to read.

Avoid Anything That's Hard To Read

Type your letter in a standard font: Times New Roman or Courier.

Include A Gimmick

The very best direct mail letters contain some sort of gimmick; something out of the ordinary that makes them memorable and interesting. A gimmick is a brilliant way to get attention, and stop people in their tracks. It's also great if you're following your letter up with a phone call.

A Special Note About Approaching Ally Businesses

The main thing to bear in mind is that you are doing the ally business a favour. If they truly understand what you're proposing, they should jump at the chance.

Here's the simplest explanation – you're giving them the chance to boost their own profits, get more customers and receive the thanks of their customers (for referring them to a quality business).

If you'd like to get paid for the referrals you give, remember that when you approach the ally businesses.

There are certain concessions you may need to make to ensure the deal happens. Here is a list of things you can offer the ally business if there's any doubt:

- **You pay for the postage:** It's your idea, so you should pay for it. The best you're likely to get is half and half. The ally may offer to drop it in with a mailing they're already doing, but you'd be better off paying for a separate mailing.

- **You pack the envelopes:** There's no reason why you should ask the business owner to do anything aside from provide the names. They may want to stick labels on so you don't get to keep the names.

- **You promise you will only use the names once:** If they do give you their list, you should probably guarantee that once this promotion's over, you won't touch the names again.

- **You will do the same thing for them:** If you're not willing to do the same for them, why should they do it for you?

Step 6: What Else (Do You Need To Think About)?

Use this section as a final checklist. Once you're happy with your strategy letter, run through and make sure you're ready to get started. Here are a few things you may have overlooked:

Team Training: Does your team fully understand the strategy you've implemented? It's important they understand the vital role they are to play in this strategy.

Objects: Have you included an item with each letter?

Check Stock and Team Levels: There would be nothing worse than having a rush of new customers come in only to find you have no stock or are too busy to serve them.

"OK Charlie, I just know you're busting to write your own now. Take a few minutes and let's see what you come up with."

"No worries, mate. I have it all worked out in my head already."

He busied himself while I stretched my legs once more. Funny how a quick walk around a workshop can be so refreshing.

This is what he wrote:

Here's a beer and a way to make more doing less.

Hi there Scott...

I know what it's like dealing with customers we both deal with - that's why I've sent a beer to cool you down after working in the hot sun.

See, I run a mechanical workshop – Charlie's Garage, you might have heard of us ... we've been around for the last 8 years.

Anyway, I've come up with an idea - a way that we can both help each other get more customers and make extra money to boot.

Before explaining anything, let me say this ... I'm writing to YOU because I've heard good things about your work. People tell me you do a professional job and leave customers smiling - exactly the type of business person I want to deal with.

The idea works like this – every time I'm working on a job and I see that the customer could use some window tinting, I'll give them your name. I've also got the same arrangement with Jimmy's Windscreens, Darren's Car Yard and Southside Boats. And each of these businesses are also willing to refer any window tinting customers to you.

All we ask is that you return the favour – every time you meet a customer who needs windscreens replacing, who might be in the market for a car or boat, or, most importantly, who could do with a service, pass them on.

Whoever spots the job gets 15% of it – which means you'll make around $150 a week, just by recommending Charlie's Garage or one of the other three businesses.

Of course, the same applies if we send a customer to you.

And just so you know, I had about three customers last week that needed window tinting. I told them to look in the Yellow Pages – but I could have just as easily sent them to you. Ultimately, I want to do some joint-promotions ... you know – get some fridge magnets and flyers out to the local area.

Imagine – five businesses, each helping the other out and sending each other customers. That's more clout than you can poke a stick at – we'll be the 'big boys'.

I'm going to phone you this afternoon to explain the idea in more depth. Expect my call about 4pm. If you're busy, I'll set up a time for us to speak on Monday.

Look forward to speaking to you soon,

Charlie
Charlie's Garage

PS Actually, this isn't really my idea – I've seen a hairdresser do it. She got together with a beauty salon, florist and gym.

Example

Template of a letter to an ally business

Good morning [NAME]

Here's a $x.00 gift you can give every one of your customers ... FREE.

I've come up with a great idea. A way that we, as business people who both deal with [target market], can help each other.

It won't cost you anything. It'll fit in with your current promotional efforts and it's guaranteed to make your current customers feel special. More importantly, it'll give them another good reason to come back and buy from you again (or recommend that their friends do).

Here's the idea ...

I manage a company called [business] – we [perform whatever service you perform]. [Back-up statement].

[Something that you believe is special or unique about you].

More on that later. First, I want to explain how this applies to you ...

People usually pay $x for us [do something]. This is [explanation of service]. I've recently had 500 x $x vouchers printed – these cover the cost of this [service]. Of course, there's no obligation to go ahead with anything, but it will give the person an idea of what's possible.

Here's where you come in ...

I'm happy for you to distribute these vouchers to your customers. They're genuinely valued at $x each. It'd make an excellent gift for your customers. I've also written a letter that I'd like you to send out with the vouchers.

Even better than that, I'm willing to pay for the postage, printing and envelopes – all you need to do is stick the address labels. I won't see the list, and won't have the opportunity to contact your customers unless they contact me.

It's a fantastic way to do something special for your customers without really doing very much at all. All you need to do is say "yes" when I call and I'll organise for everything to go ahead.

And remember – this promotion won't cost you anything, and is a brilliant, meaningful way to treat your past customers.

I'll call you in the next few days, just to answer any questions you have, and to organise the finer details ...

Look forward to speaking with you then,

[name]

[business name]

PS [commission incentive]

$$\boxed{\textbf{Part 6}}$$

▌Referral Strategies

"We're now going to go one step further, Charlie. Until now, we've been looking at ways of generating leads ourselves – through various forms of advertising – and we've been looking at ways to get other businesses to generate leads for us. What other way is there to generate leads?"

"You've got me there, Brad. Isn't that all there are?"

"No, there's one other very important and powerful source of leads and that's your very own customers."

"Ah, how stupid of me. How could I have forgotten them? You're always reminding me to keep the customer in mind, but it never occurred to me they could actually bring in more business, other than their own."

"Don't worry, Charlie – you're not the only one, I can assure you. So here's what we're going to do. We're going to look at various ways we can tap into your customer base and get it to work for you."

What Is A Referral Strategy?

A referral strategy is a way of introducing new customers to your business for a low acquisition cost. Basically, it's a way of getting your existing customers to promote your business for you. A way of getting them to introduce their family, friends and colleagues to your product or service.

What Makes A Successful Referral Strategy?

There are a number of elements which when combined, make a successful referral strategy. These range from finding the right type of customer, to the strategy that best suits your type of business. There are two things you need to understand above all else:

Service

Your service must be extraordinary. Having good or even great service just won't do. If you want people to refer their friends, then make sure your service is first-rate.

Your Offer

If you don't give people a good reason, a 'What's in it for me?', your strategy will fail. Some of the strategies you'll discover in the next section will rely on your offer more heavily than others, but regardless of which one you choose, always ask yourself this: "Would I refer someone for that reason?"

In the following pages you'll learn how to put a referral strategy into place. Which type suits which business, the types of customers you want to refer you, and those you'd rather didn't.

The 5 Steps To Creating A Killer Referral Strategy

Step 1: Why (Use A Referral Strategy)?

Before deciding on the type of referral strategy (there are a number to choose from), you need to work out whether this is the right overall strategy for you. You need to compare its potential returns to other ways you could use to market yourself.

Whilst a referral strategy has a low hard dollar cost, some can be quite time consuming.

A referral strategy is ideal when you have a higher priced product or service. Whilst almost any type of business can benefit from having a referral strategy (or a number of them for that matter), there are some businesses it doesn't suit quite as well. For example, it's probably inappropriate for a fast food outlet as these businesses tend to too many customers at any one time.

Having said that, a strategy where your customers could take a card or a flyer and pass it on to their friends, could work quite well. You could also have an offer for groups of four or more.

Of course, a referral strategy is an ideal backup for your existing marketing. If you've invested money to get a new client to come in, why not get them to bring their friends? It can, of course, work well as a stand-alone strategy.

Step 2: Who (Is Your Target Market)?

Before you even embark on a referral strategy, you need to decide the type of customers you want to do business with. The last thing you want is to get referrals who don't translate into business. You know, the ones who only buy off you once and never do business with you again, or even worse, those who create more headaches than they do sales, and never give you the business you're after.

If you don't set the rules, your new customers will set them for you. So you must decide who your ideal customer is. Some customers are more trouble than they're worth. They'll actually cost you money. The 80:20 rule, sometimes called the Pareto Principle, states that 20 % of your business comes from 80% of your customers. The other side of this is that 80% of your headaches will generally come from 20% of your customers.

So, before you rush out to get more new customers, decide on the type of people you want as new customers. You also need to grade your existing customers in one of four categories; either A, B, C or D.

An example of an A-grade customer is someone who pays their bills on time, is pleasant to deal with, is happy to pay your marked prices, send their friends to you, and spends a reasonable amount with you each year.

Don't put up with customers who won't pay their bills, don't treat you well and constantly hassle you on price. These customers will generally refer similar types of people, and that's the last thing you want to happen. To get rid of your D-grade customers (those you don't want to do business with), simply send them a letter asking them to deal with someone else. You can't afford to deal with them any more.

Your C's will meet just one or two or your criteria and need to be sent a fairly strong letter that informs them of the new rules of doing business with you.

Some will abide by the new rules; others will want to go elsewhere. Either way, once you've moved all your 'C' and 'D' customers out, your next step will be to train your B-grade customers how to be in the A-grade with a simple letter. Every client will now be aware of the type of customers you want to deal with. The most important message you need to get through as you send out these letters is you're doing it to be able to provide the best service possible for your target market.

Step 3: What (Are You Offering)?

You need to teach your customers why it's good for them to give referrals. People will generally only do something for you if you give them a good reason to. Your customers want to know why they should do things for you; they want to know how they'll be affected when they take action and most of all, what they will get in return.

When you're being pro-active about getting referrals, you need to take all this into account, even if all they get in return is the knowledge that they've helped a friend find what they need.

You'll have to educate them about how referring people to you can, and will, help them. We'll get into the rewards you can give later but for now, just tell them the simple logic I've used so many times for success before.

Referal Strategies

Your customers will benefit in several ways by referring people to you. Let me list them for you:

- By referring you new clients, they're helping you save marketing dollars and that allows you to pass on greater savings to them, greater rewards, or better service.

- They're making sure you have a strong and healthy business, so you're around in the future when they might need you again.

- They're helping you work with only the best clients so you can always come up with new ways of serving them better ... and so on ...

Every time you educate one customer about referring new people to you, you've got an advocate for life ... with one condition. And that is you always give them the level of service you've promised. It doesn't have to be 5 star, just what you've promised.

Another quick tip about educating people how to refer: be sure to let them know you're after quality people, just like them. You'll give them a compliment and set a standard for whom they refer to you straight away.

Step 4: How (Are You Going To Encourage Referrals)?

Once you know whom you want to deal with, and what you're prepared to offer to get them in through the door, the next step is working out your strategy.

Referral strategies can be the trickiest of them all. You are asking people to risk something that is dearly important to them ... the respect of their friends. That may sound a little over the top, but consider this example: let's say you convince a friend to buy a car that turns out to be a dud. How is that friend going to feel about you?

Or what if your friend's appearance was completely destroyed by a hairdresser you recommended.

The negative effects can vary in intensity, but there is always a risk. If you tell someone to do something and it turns into a nightmare, you can expect some of the fallout. Of course, the reverse is also true. If you introduce a friend to a business that solves a problem for them, or gives them exactly the service they've been looking for, it can reflect very positively on you.

People tend to highly value what other people think of them. That means, they won't refer someone to you unless they're absolutely sure they won't be embarrassed, or be blamed for anything going wrong.

The upshot of this: if your service or products aren't up to scratch, you can forget about referrals. Get that part right, and you'll get more referrals than ever.

Once you feel comfortable that people are happy with your service and products, you can start work on some specific referral-generating strategies.

The following is a list of different strategies you can use to get more referrals. You'll find examples at the end of this section. Make a mark next to any you feel would suit your business. And remember, there's no reason you have to choose just one – why not do three or four? Your customers may think it's a little strange, but they're unlikely to mind (especially if you have awesome service).

Importantly, you must test and measure – don't be afraid to kill something that isn't working. Then have another look through the list and try something else. Keep doing this until you find the strategy that works for your business.

Now, onto that list:

Call And Ask To Mail Your Customers' Friends A Special Offer

This is a strategy that almost always produces results, especially for businesses where purchases are few and far between.

First, write your past customers a letter which says something along these lines: 'Hi there, just wanted to let you know about a special offer we're making right now. Obviously, you won't be that interested – you just bought a couple of months ago. But what about your friends? I'd like to mail your two closest buddies $50 to spend with us. I'll give you a call in the next few days to get their details."

Three days later, you phone and say, "Hi, just following-up on that letter we sent you last week. Do you remember receiving it? Did you understand it? Who was the first person that sprung to mind when you read it? And what's their address?"

Next, you write the friend a letter. Use a great headline, something like this: "Here's why George Matthews suggested I write to tell you about our winter special." Of course, you just substitute the name of the referee and the title of the special (introductory, spring madness, summer, New Year, etc).

You'll find the person will DEFINITELY read every word. More than that, they'll immediately phone their friend. The friend will then sell your business for you – "Yeah, they're really good to deal with – and that's a great special ... that's cheaper than I got mine for."

Next, you call the referred friend and book an appointment for them to see your showroom or quote, whichever is applicable.

Use A Referral Price

This is a brilliant way to stimulate immediate referrals with every sale. At the point when the person is about to pay for your product or service, ask them this question:

Referal Strategies

"Thanks for choosing us [name], and by the way, would you like the referral or non-referral price?"

Naturally, the buyer will respond something like this: "What's the difference?"

To answer, use a standard script such as this: "Well [name], we're aware a lot of our business comes from people telling other people. For that, we reward those who recommend their friends to us. If you know two people who might be interested in buying a [product], and you give us their contact details, we give you the referral price – that's about 10% less."

People will usually jump at the chance, unless they don't know anyone. And the referrals will generally be good ones. Only D class clients will attempt to give you dodgy leads. The majority of people will give it some real thought, and may even call their friends to put in a good word.

The referral price idea works best when it is applied as standard practice and used without fear. If people sense that you are uncomfortable with the idea, they will be too. If, however, you make it obvious this is the way you do business, they'll go with the flow and give you the names.

Do Regular Mail-Outs Offering An Incentive

A simple idea that can be effective, if done correctly. Here's what you do:

Mail your customers, starting the letter something like this: "Hi there. Just wanted to write and say thanks - thanks for choosing [business name]."

After the preamble, get to the point. "We're aware many of our customers come from referrals, that is, happy customers recommending their friends visit us."

Then ask for the referral directly. "If you know anyone who's currently in the market, I ask that you give them one of the referral cards I've included. Thanks [name], and I look forward to seeing you again soon."

In your PS, offer a sweetener ... "By the way, if one of your friends brings their card in and buys any time in the next 21 days, I'll post you a small gift – a voucher for a FREE massage."

If the incentive is exciting, you'll find referrals will flow in. Best of all, it's generally very easy to get the incentive for free. In the above example, it would be simple to call the local masseur, and ask for a couple of hundred free vouchers. Any switched-on masseur would understand the lifetime value of a new client.

To make the strategy more effective again, it's a good idea to follow-up the letters with a phone call. Use questions such as this: "Who was the first person you thought of handing a card to?"

Give Top Service

If you treat your customers well, they'll refer their friends in massive quantities – that much is clear. But what about really going the extra mile – doing things your customers would never expect?

Here are a couple of examples:

- A sandwich bar that painted caricatures of their regular customers and hung them on the wall. The best part was that the customer had no idea until after the picture had been hung. You can imagine how that got them talking.

- A photocopier salesman who mailed a free gift to his past customers every month. First was a massage, next a haircut, then a dinner for two. He did this every month for a year. Needless to say, his number of referrals went up dramatically.

- A car salesman who mailed one card every month to every person who'd ever bought from him – birthday, Christmas, Easter, Valentines and so on.

These are just three examples of AWESOME service – extra special touches that really get customers talking to their friends. You can just imagine someone saying over dinner: "... and this sandwich bar I always go to, they drew a picture of me and put it on the wall – and the food's really good too!"

What can you do to really excite your customers?

Hold A *'Bring A Friend'* Closed-Door Sale

Closed-door sales always work well. The promise of great bargains, combined with the feeling of being special, is particularly enticing. But what about spicing up the idea with this strategy?

Make the price of entry a friend. That's right – if people want to get in, they have to bring one person that has never bought from your business before. And that applies to EVERY person who comes along.

Naturally, you have to make the sale exciting – offer some great limited deals and exclusive viewings of the latest product. Drinks, nibblies and entertainment will help make it more attractive again. And if you want to really get people in, offer an expensive give-away ... a TV, holiday or house-full of carpet.

Of course, make sure you get the name, address and phone number of every 'friend' who comes along. Mail to them shortly after, offering them an introductory special.

Referal Strategies

Ask The Question

Ever heard the saying 'who dares wins'? In business it's exactly the same. There's no reason why you can't ask your customers for referrals any time.

You don't need a strategy or letter – just phone them and say, "I was just wondering whether you know anyone in the market for [product] right now –we're running a special promotion and I thought I'd give your friends the chance to take it up first."

Of course, you could do the same thing with people who drop into your store, or who have just bought.

Here's one of the more interesting applications of the idea. Ask people who go through the sales process yet don't buy. That is, those who think about buying from you, but eventually say no.

Here's an example: Mary is thinking about buying a patio, so she calls Jim's Home Improvements. After a quote and much discussion, she works out she can't afford it. Jim, following up the quote he sent out, asks: "What did you decide?" Mary replies, "Jim, the patio looks lovely, but I just can't afford it now."

She feels guilt at this point and is eager to make it up to Jim in some way. Jim knows this, so as quick as a flash, he says: "That's a shame Mary. I think the design we've come up with is really attractive, and would look great in your back yard." Mary agrees. Then Jim continues, "That's OK, Mary – how many people do you know who are also thinking about building a patio at the moment?"

Mary might say one or two, which leads perfectly into Jim's next question: "Who was the first person that sprung to mind? And what's their phone number?"

Mail Out VIP Cards To Your Customers, And Include A Couple Of Extras

VIP loyalty cards are brilliant for two reasons. Firstly, they give your customers good reason to buy from you more often. Secondly, they 'tie them up' – in other words, protect them from being stolen by competitors. Every time the customer considers 'straying', you want them to ask themselves this: "Why go to them when I get all this great stuff from my regular guys?"

The great stuff has to be great. Just offering a 10% discount is a bit weak, unless the product is super-expensive. Try every 6th purchase free, or a free gift each time they buy.

To introduce the card to your customers, write them a letter that explains the benefits of being a VIP card member and why they've been chosen. Something like: "I've only mailed this card to my top customers" usually works wonders.

To get referrals, add a PS that says: "You'll notice I've included a couple of extra VIP cards. Please give it some thought and hand these to two people you believe would appreciate them."

Encourage Your Current Customers To Buy Gift Vouchers

This is a brilliant way to make more sales AND get referrals. Here's a great application of this idea:

Write a letter to your customers and offer them a special deal – if they buy a gift voucher in the next 21 days, you'll add 20% value on top ... FREE!!! For example, if they buy a gift voucher for $100, you'll write it out to the value of $120.

The only condition is the recipient must be someone new to the store and their name and address must be on the gift voucher. Of course, you get to keep the details on file as well.

Hold A Party To Celebrate Your Customer Buying From You - And Invite Their Friends

This is probably the best (and most fun) referral strategy there is. It works brilliantly with new homes, or home improvement products.

Here's how it works:

After the customer buys, write them a letter that says: "Thanks for buying from us – and we hope you're delighted with every aspect of your new [x].

To celebrate, we'd like to throw you a party ... and cover the costs! I'll call you tomorrow and get the names of people you'd like to invite and a date and time that suits."

You call, get the names and addresses, and then mail invitations. Of course, in the process you're gathering details of possible referrals. You pay for drinks and nibblies and organise the party. This, in itself, will create great feelings and generate referrals.

To take the idea to the next level, show up half way through with some extra drinks. While you're there, introduce yourself and network. You'll be amazed by the results, and the number of people who say: "Oh, you're the [x] seller. I've been thinking about buying an [x] for years."

Let Your Customers Know In Advance You'll Be Asking For Referrals

Before you've sold anything, you can let your customers know you'll be expecting referrals.

" Well [NAME] ... before we get into what it is you need, I'd just like to let you know how we work with our customers. Would that be OK?" Then follow it up with this: "We get about 80% of our business from referrals and I like to work with people like yourself. So, what I'd like to ask is that if you believe you get value from working with me, you'll refer at least two people to me who are just like yourself. I'm not asking you for them now, but at some stage I'll ask you for them. Would that be OK?"

You may even find that by giving it to them and then taking it away, they may want to give you some referrals up front.

Another simple tool to use here is to leave a form with your new customers on which they can fill out their referrals. Then you tell them that you'll be back to pick up their referrals in a couple of weeks.

Make Giving Referrals A Condition Of Doing Business With You.

If you really want to have a business that runs on just referrals, then make it a rule. You can introduce your 'referral rule' using a set of Commitment Statements.

These set out what you'll do for your customers and then asks them to make certain commitments to you in return. One could be something like this: "You agree to give us three referrals every year."

You could even put an audiotape together that outlines how you work with your new clients. You could only accept clients who are referred to you by your current customers. They should already know the rules of doing business with you. If you're going to do this, you need to make sure your business is genuinely giving **AWESOME** service from the moment a client contacts you. It's also important your customers aren't in competition with each other.

Putting On A Seminar For Your Past Clients And Asking Them To Invite Their Friends

The secret here is to either bring in an expert your customers will know and respect, or pick a topic they've been trying to find information about.

Be sure to invite at least five or ten times the number of people you want to attend and book a room that looks full with the number of prospects you expect to get.

Go for quality at the seminar, a good venue, a good speaker and nice refreshments. Give people a chance to ask questions on the night and make sure they have the option of buying. And absolutely make sure you get everyone's name and details.

When you do the speaking yourself, get either a local newspaper or your industry magazine to cover the event and take photos for your own customer newsletter.

Structure the seminar so it's about 90% information and 10% selling. The idea is to position yourself as the expert, not the best sales person. People love to buy from experts as the trust level is much higher.

Step 5: What Else (Do You Need To Think About)?

Use this section as a final checklist – once you're happy with the referral system you've chosen, run through and make sure you're ready to get started. Here are a few things you may not have thought of:

Team Training

Does your team fully understand the strategy you've implemented? It's important they understand the vital role they are to play in it. If your newly referred customers come in and find anything less than the level of service you've promised, your strategy will fail.

Gifts

Have you organised the gifts or vouchers you've offered as incentives for people who refer their friends? You must ensure your existing customers receive the product you promised. Ensure you have an ample supply of printed vouchers or gifts in stock and that they're sent on time.

Check Stock And Team Levels

It's unlikely your strategy will bring in hundreds of people all at once, but if it does, you need to be prepared. Plan for your strategy by making sure you cater for any increased demand.

Charlie was, once again, raring to go. I could see he already had in mind the basis of what he wanted to do. So I left him to it, not wanting to dampen his enthusiasm. I needn't have worried.

"What do you think of this, Brad," he said, handing me his hand-written note. I reckon it'll work a treat. You see, personal recommendation is a big factor in my game. After all, if you're entrusting your pride and joy to someone you don't know, wouldn't you prefer to deal with someone you had a handle on? That's the way I see it, anyway."

"You're dead right, mate," I continued, and began to read.

Here's why Brad Sugars recommended I write and tell you about Charlie's Garage ...

Good morning Jane ...

I was speaking to Brad the other day and your name came up.

He and I were talking about how you could benefit from what he has to offer. From what Brad was saying, it'd be perfect for your situation.

I don't think Brad would mind if I revealed that he has saved over $1,200 on his last service.

I've set aside some time this week to talk to you about it. I have an hour put aside on Thursday at 1pm, or Friday at 3pm. I'll call you in a few days time to work out which of these times would suit you best.

Look forward to speaking with you then ...

Charlie
Charlie's Garage

PS I specialise in European sports cars, so if you book your Porsche in for a service this month, I'll give it to you for half the normal price – guaranteed.

Referral Card

This is a basic template of a referral card that you can give your customers. It is advisable however, to have your cards professionally produced by a printer. You might like to use the templates below as an example for your printer to base a design on. You should also include your logo and perhaps a background colour to make the card stand out.

(Your Company Name)

Referral Card

Your company address

Telephone Number

Mobile

Fax number

Place your special conditions here

Name: . . . .

Address: . . . .

. . . .

Phone: B/H . . . .

Phone: A/H . . . .

Referred by: . . . .

Part 7

■ Unique Selling Proposition And Guarantee

"Charlie, we're now going to discover your competitive advantage, uniqueness, and use them to develop a strong guarantee."

"Great, Brad. I think I have something I'd call unique, if you know what I mean. But don't let me interrupt."

I love an interactive client, and Charlie was proving to be a great learner. He wasn't afraid to probe new concepts and question that, which he was having difficulty with.

"What I'm talking about here is more than good service or a good price; it's all about knowing what it is that makes you special and being able to specifically explain this to your customers."

"Yeah, I know what you mean. You're on about a point of difference, aren't you?"

"That's basically it. It's what I call your unique selling proposition, or USP for short. It's the thing that sets you apart from your competitors."

Charlie's experience and situation is no different to thousands of others. He struggles with the same constraints and challenges that face just about every other business owner. So as a reader of this book, you'll identify with much of what he's going through as he tried to strike a balance between working ON his business and working IN it. Take over from Charlie from here on in and see how you'd fare going through the rest of this exercise.

Once you've read through this section of the book, you should know exactly what it is that makes you unique. You may discover there is nothing that makes you unique at all. But that's where the real fun begins. You see, you'll get to rethink your business, to look at it from outside the box. You'll then be able to INVENT a uniqueness.

You'll also have a full guarantee, written down exactly as it should be. This guarantee will be powerful. It will stop your potential customers dead in their tracks. The guarantee is heavily linked to your USP; in fact it can be the same thing. For example, if you run a funeral parlour that guarantees everyone will be smiling by the end of the funeral, you'd have a pretty attention-grabbing USP right there.

121

This is the next step in your marketing success story. From this point on, you'll have a real point of difference, and you'll know how to use it. That I can personally guarantee.

What Is A Successful USP And Guarantee?

To begin with, it's important to know how to define a successful USP and guarantee. You see, if you don't know what you're aiming for, you'll never know if the whole exercise has been worth the trouble.

So, perhaps a better place to start is deciding what an UN-successful strategy one is. Here are a couple of rough guidelines:

- You finish writing it then stash it away in your filing cabinet forever.
- You do use it but nobody notices or cares.
- There are already three competitors out there with the same guarantee and uniqueness.
- Your USP and guarantee doesn't target something your customers care about. For example, a hairdresser who guarantees to sweep up your hair before you leave. They want to be known as the 'clean floor' hairdresser. No one cares!

Ok, now you know what a weak USP and guarantee is, it's easy to work out what a good one is.

For a start, it has to have IMPACT. It needs to make people sit up and take notice and it has to get them thinking and talking. A great example is a restaurant that has no menu. They just cook whatever you feel like and they guarantee to cook it better than your mother would! Now that would get attention.

What about your business? You need to think of aspects of your service that make a difference to people. This will be covered in more depth shortly, but I want you to start thinking about it now. Your uniqueness needs to tackle your competitors head on and your guarantee needs to answer the most common frustration your customers have.

What Makes A Successful USP And Guarantee?

There are a number of elements that make a big difference when creating a strong USP and guarantee. Follow these guidelines to the letter and you'll be set. Let's tackle USP and guarantees separately, shall we?

These are broad guidelines only and are designed to get you in the right mode of thinking. I'll be giving you a lot more specific information shortly.

A successful USP should be:

- Truly unique.
- Exciting to your target market.
- Something that will get people talking.
- Something that can't be easily copied, or if it can be, it will be an obvious rip-off on the part of the offending business.

A successful and powerful guarantee should be:

- Specific.
- Something that addresses the main frustrations and fears of customers when dealing with your industry.
- Be complete. It should say 'either this happens or we'll do this.'
- Impressive.

Now of course, it's a tall order to do all that, especially if you're in a mature industry where most angles have already been tackled. Sometimes it pays to get an outsider's perspective. Chances are, you're probably too wrapped up in your own business to see it as an outsider would. Just ask a person on the street what they would you like to see a business in your industry offer.

When you come up with a few opinions, don't think about why they can't be done – give some thought to how it CAN be done.

The 7 Steps To Creating Powerful USPs And Guarantees

Step 1: Why (Do You Need A USP)?

The following paragraphs may really make you think, and hopefully answer some questions you've had about business for years.

So many business owners beat their heads against the wall, wondering why their business isn't working. They try everything – new sales scripts, better ads, new products, yet all to no avail ... every day they open their doors, they plunge further into debt.

In most cases, the reason things aren't working is very simple – there's not enough business out there, and very little reason for anyone to give it to you instead of your competitors.

To illustrate my point, think about this example. Harry and Barry open up a hardware store. There are six other hardware stores in the immediate area, but the boys aren't fazed as they believe pimply kids who don't know anything staff the other shops. According to Harry and Barry, they're experts in the game – and will get heaps of business simply because of that.

They open a store a block down from the big competitor, write a couple of ads with the headline 'Opening Sale' and they're off and running. For two weeks, things seem to go well. They may be selling the products extra cheap, but they're selling lots. The cash register keeps ringing and things are pumping along.

Soon though, things slow down. In fact, they almost come to a dead stop. Just a few customers a day, buying a hammer here and some nails there. The boys wonder why.

Whilst they did get a few things right – the ads were OK, the customer service was good, the store was well laid out and the products were well chosen – they missed the most important point of all ... whether the business was viable in the first pace. If they'd done a little research first, they would have discovered the following: every year, 1.1 million dollars is spent on hardware in their area. If each of the seven local hardware stores had an equal share of sales, each one would have a turnover of around $150,000.

Of course, the stores had wildly different figures. The largest, a nationwide chain had the lion's share at $475,000 – almost half. The next biggest, a smaller, older store with a loyal client base, had $260,000. The five others made up the rest. Naturally, four of them were on the verge of going under. The fifth was Harry and Barry's.

Looking at it from this perspective, the boys' dream of opening a hardware store and becoming wealthy seemed a little unrealistic. They'll be lucky if they last the next six months.

Think about your situation. How much business is out there, and how much can you actually claim?

If the total market is only worth a million dollars, and you manage to grab 10% of it, that's only $100,000 turnover. Take out basic expenses (not including your own wage), and you'd be lucky to pull $30,000 profit. You may as well go and work for someone else. That way, you'll earn more money and have less responsibility. If the business goes down, it's not your house, car and credit rating that's on the line.

Remember, if you don't have a good reason for people to come to you, then you'll get lost in the crowd.

It's always amazing to see another small strip shopping centre open up, especially when there are already five or six others within ten minutes of each other and there are two major shopping centres nearby. The strip centre as a whole has no uniqueness and therefore it has no reason for existence. The best it could probably do is promote the fact that they're small and new. That's not really good enough. 'Small' usually means more expensive and 'new' means nothing.

So what about your business? When you started, did you begin with a uniqueness – a real point of difference, or did you just start as a 'me too' competitor?

Here's an interesting thought and something that most new business owners never consider. When a new grocery store opens up, it has to share sales with all other grocery stores in the area. If there are already three stores and two of them are already struggling, what makes you think the new one will have a better chance?

All that's been done is to split the existing sales further. Now, instead of the total areas grocery sales being split between three, they have to be split between four. If the business was started as a 'me too' business, you can forget it. The days of competing on price and service are beginning to end. These days, people have so many options; they can almost always get it somewhere cheaper, from someone who'll do it better.

My major point is clear – you must STAND OUT. If you have no uniqueness, you have no reason for existence. Remember that – as new competitors come into the market, you'll continue to sink. If there's no reason for people to continue coming to you and not them, you'll keep losing customers. It's a gloomy forecast, but a realistic one.

You must work out your uniqueness, and you must do it NOW.

Step 2: Why (Do You Need A Guarantee)?

People have been burned before. They've used products that they were told fantastic things about, only to be bitterly disappointed.

You must take that risk away for them.

To understand how and why, you need to understand this: When customers buy, they are not buying your product or service ... they are buying the benefit of owning or experiencing whatever it is you sell.

For example, people don't buy lawnmowers; they are buying a lawn that is properly mowed and the feeling of being house-proud that comes with it.

Another example; Customers don't buy food; they buy satisfaction, survival and the pleasure of eating. In the case of a restaurant, they are also buying an experience and a social occasion.

If you guarantee to give people the benefit they are after in the first place, there is a high probability they'll want to deal with you.

Imagine a hairdresser that had a special guarantee for every single person who got their haircut on Saturday morning. The guarantee read like this: "If you don't look the best you ever have on Saturday night and get three times as much interest from the opposite sex, we will pay for you to see another hairdresser."

Remember, people aren't buying a haircut; they're buying a look and the feeling of looking their best. I could go really deep into psychology here – people want to look their best because they want acceptance. They want acceptance because they want to feel good about themselves. They want to feel good about themselves because they want to feel as though they are a worthwhile person, which is one of the most basic human needs.

Phew! I bet the hairdresser thought she was just cutting hair. It's important to bear in mind you are selling more than just the product. If people are unsure they will get the main benefit from dealing with you, they may hesitate when it comes to actually buying, or they may buy from someone else who makes them feel more secure.

It's all about understanding what makes the customer tick, then absolutely guaranteeing to give them that. If they don't feel they have received what you promised, they get compensation. When people feel as though they have nothing to lose, they are more likely to buy or take action. Most action is delayed forever, simply because people are afraid of what will happen if they make a mistake.

Imagine if every customer who came to you thought, "Well, I can't lose with these guys. I'll buy it now and see how it works out."

A guarantee can get you around a lot of the sales process too. If people already feel certain they will get what they set out to get, they will be less worried about spending time obsessing over every detail.

If there's ever a problem, they know they can come back and get a refund. Of course, you need to make sure the product you are recommending to people is the right one for their needs. And naturally, if your product or service isn't up to scratch, a guarantee may kill your business.

However, if 98% of your customers are happy and you are satisfied with your product or service, then guarantee away. If people always seem to be happy, why not guarantee that they will be.

A Myth About Guarantees

Many people are frightened of guarantees. They honestly think customers will rip them off. The truth is that most guarantees are never taken advantage of, even when the customer is genuinely dissatisfied.

There are two reasons why. Firstly, people are lazy and couldn't be bothered. Secondly, it takes a lot of confidence to stand up and say, "Hey, I'm not happy. Give me my money back."

The fact is, most people lack this confidence. That's not to say there aren't people out there who will rip you off – you'll get the occasional pathetic person who buys an item, uses it a couple of times, then returns it, for no other reason than it's already served it's purpose. These people know they are doing the wrong thing and have a sense of guilt.

If you prick that guilt, they'll usually go away. When they phone to tell you they want to return something, ask some very direct questions. "So what is it you don't like about the item?" "How many times have you used it?" "So what are you going to buy instead?"

Make sure the person is returning the item so they can buy something else – your guarantee should not cater for people who buy things they don't need and can't afford. If you ask these questions, many of them will back off. There's nothing wrong with making them work for their refund either. Why not get them to fill out a three-page feedback form, explaining what the problems were, along with all their personal details. Encourage them to take it away and fill it out at home.

The people with genuine problems will come back with the form, the rest will see it as too hard.

Of course, these customers are the last thing to worry about - your new powerful guarantee will bring you more customers overall, so it's worth taking that small chance.

Step 3: Who (Is Your Target Market)?

Before you start getting right into the details of your uniqueness and guarantee, you need to identify exactly whom it is you're trying to impress.

Precisely who is your target market?

A failure to answer this question will lead to failure FOREVER. For example, imagine a company who sells in-ground swimming pools positioning themselves as the renter's specialist and guaranteeing the fastest service in winter. The target market would not care, as people who buy swimming pools own their own homes and buy in spring or summer!

Knowing your target market will also enable you to communicate better with them. So let's get specific. Who are the people most likely to be interested in your product or service? Here are some guidelines:

Age: How old are they?

Sex: Are they male or female?

Income: How much do they make?

Where do they live: Are they local, or do they come from miles around to deal with you?

Step 4: What (Makes You Unique)?

The best way to discover your uniqueness is to start looking at your business from the outside.

The following questions will help you find out what it is that makes you unique, and will help you think about your business in a new way. Be sure to be honest, and to spend the time giving detailed answers. Don't cheat yourself! Take the time and get your answers down in detail.

List your three biggest competitors.

1 . . . .

2 . . . .

3 . . . .

What do they do well?

1 . . . .

2 . . . .

3 . . . .

What do they do poorly?

1 . . . .

2 . . . .

3 . . . .

What would the average person say about each of these competitors?

1 . . . .

2 . . . .

3 . . . .

What is 'unique' about them?

1 . . . .

2 . . . .

3 . . . .

What can they do that you can't?

1 ....

2 ....

3 ....

Where are they geographically located in comparison to you and your potential market place?

1 ....

2 ....

3 ....

Describe the perceived standards of customer service in your industry.

....

....

....

Describe the perceived standards of technology in your industry.

....

....

....

Describe the perceived standards of product quality in your industry.

....

....

....

Describe the perceived standards in sales & marketing in your industry.

....

....

....

Unique Selling Proposition And Guarantee

How does your business compare to these industry standards?

Customer Service . . . .

. . . .

. . . .

Technology . . . .

. . . .

. . . .

Product Quality . . . .

. . . .

. . . .

Sales and Marketing . . . .

. . . .

. . . .

. . . .

If there was one phrase your customers and prospects used to describe what you do NOW, it would be ...

"OH, you're the guys who ...."

. . . .

. . . .

. . . .

. . . .

. . . .

If there was one phrase your customers and prospects used to describe what you do in an IDEAL WORLD, it would be ...

"OH, you're the guys who ...."

. . . .

. . . .

. . . .

. . . .

. . . .

What are four reasons your customers come to you rather than your competitors? This question is especially important, so give it some real thought.

1 . . . .

2 . . . .

3 . . . .

4 . . . .

In what four ways do you perceive you are genuinely different from your competitors?

1 . . . .

2 . . . .

3 . . . .

4 . . . .

What are five things about your product or service that you take for granted, yet your customers don't know about?

1 . . . .

2 . . . .

3 . . . .

4 . . . .

5 . . . .

OK, now you've been through all that, you should have a much better idea of what sets you apart from your competitors. Now it's time to ask yourself whether this uniqueness really matters to your customers. So what if you're a stationery store with the biggest range of pencil sharpeners? People aren't that interested!

Unique Selling Proposition And Guarantee

Out of the unique points you've identified, which is the most marketable? Which point will appeal most to your customers? Here are some examples of what your uniqueness could be ...

You sell a higher quality product or service, and you can specifically show how it benefits the customer in a meaningful way.

You provide more/better customer service and you can easily explain and promote why you're better.

You offer a better/longer guarantee and you have it written down.

You offer more choice/selection/options and this is something people want and always look for.

You offer a trade-in program and no-one else does.

You serve a specific (yet sizable) demographic group that is overlooked by most competitors.

You offer a better/more generous bonus points or loyalty club system and your product or service is at least as good.

You offer better value for money overall.

You have the best after sales service and this is something that you can explain to people easily when they buy.

Your product or service has unique features people care about.

You have super cheap products and services that cater for people who want the most basic thing available.

You have ultra expensive products and services that cater for those who only want the best and will pay anything to have it.

You only deal with a set number of customers, and only those of a particular type.

You offer attractive products or services that no-one else does.

You have a 'special ingredient'.

You install and deliver for free.

You bring the goods to the customer and let them choose in their own home.

You send a video catalogue, take the order over the phone and deliver within a set time period.

You have a 'one-price' approach - everything in your store is one price, regardless of what it is.

You run an ongoing competition, such as every 13th customer wins $50.

The atmosphere of your store is completely unlike anything else, either in terms of its tranquility or activity.

Your staff are all of a certain type, age group, background or experience level.

You are the fastest and guarantee to finish the job much quicker than anyone else.

Surely, amongst all of the above, you can find something you are currently doing that is unique, or more likely, something you SHOULD be doing that would make you unique.

Basically, your uniqueness comes from one of seven areas – quality, price, service, delivery, speed, convenience, and experience.

In case you're wondering, experience means the actual experience of buying from you. Imagine a video store that has four 11-foot screens that constantly play the latest releases, and live entertainment all day and night. That would be a real experience.

Once you've decided on your uniqueness, it's time to write it down. This is important because your USP will soon be communicated to your team and your customers. It needs to be summed up by a one or two line statement. Think 'Always Coca Cola' or 'Toyota: Oh, What a feeling'. Of course, your USP doesn't have to be something that sounds like it came straight from the brain of an advertising guru.

There's nothing wrong with this USP· 'Jim's Video – the only video store in Sydney with four 11-foot screens playing the latest releases and all day live entertainment.'

Just state your uniqueness plainly and simply. How about this one: 'Marie's hairdressing – where colours, streaks and perms are half the price and twice the quality.' Or 'Sally's industrial safety equipment – 456 different items always in stock and delivery is free.'

It's great to be specific. If you can put a number in your USP, then that's ideal. Think about '11 herbs and spices', or the '32 flavours'. These are USP's that stick in your mind. A beautician could say, 'Beauty Shoppe: 4 qualified and friendly beauticians with more than 23 years experience each.' Here are a couple of longer examples. It may be an idea to write your USP in a long form first, then pick out the best bits to turn it into one short and punchy sentence.

Unique Selling Proposition And Guarantee

Broad Selection

You'll always find 142 different Widgets in no less than 12 sizes and 10 exciting colours in prices ranging from $6 to $600.

You'll enjoy five times the selection, four times the colour choice, three times the number of convenient locations, twice the warranty and half the mark-up of any other dealer.

Most service companies work from 9 to 5. You'll be excited to hear we work 24 hours per day to serve you when you need it.

Discount Price

$15,000 swimming pools cost $9,850 at ABC Pool Co.

We sell the same brands of Widgets as Company X or Company Y – at 25% - 75% less.

Service Oriented

When you buy a book from us, you have a 90-day 100% money back guarantee, just in case it's not what the critics made it out to be.

When you invest in a computer system with us, you get on-site placement, FREE consultation and the security of 24-hour a day software and hardware support.

If you're looking for a plumber who is guaranteed to arrive on time and cleans up after himself, then call Joe.

Snob Appeal

Only 1,200 Widgets are produced each year. We have one put aside for you.

Mass-market gyms have up to 10,000 members, all jostling between 6am and 9pm for time on the Nautilus Machines, trying to squeeze onto the aerobics floor and queuing for the squash courts. At Club XYZ, we have a strictly limited membership of 525 families.

Now, it's time to write yours. Don't worry too much about the wording; just get the point across. If you show it to people and they don't seem to understand, you may want to rethink it. If they seem to get the idea immediately, you're on the right track.

Step 5: What (Should You Guarantee)?

Again, the easiest way to get started here is to answer a few questions, just to get you thinking. To come up with a powerful guarantee, you need to know what your customers want you to guarantee and what you actually can promise.

The idea is to match your abilities with your customers' wants. Often, it's a good idea to over promise. You probably under estimate your product or service anyway. If you think it's good, why not promise that it will be great - it'll make you pick up your act, and probably be more in line with your current customers' perceptions anyway.

Here Are The Questions:

What is your current guarantee?

. . . .

. . . .

. . . .

. . . .

What are three problems or frustrations solved by buying your product or service?

. . . .

. . . .

. . . .

. . . .

What are the three major benefits of buying your product or service?

1 . . . .

2 . . . .

3 . . . .

What frustrations do customers experience when trying to find your product or service?

. . . .

. . . .

. . . .

. . . .

. . . .

. . . .

What frustrations do customers experience when making a decision whether to buy your product or services or not?

. . . .

. . . .

. . . .

. . . .

. . . .

. . . .

What frustrations do customers experience when they set out to buy your product or service?

. . . .

. . . .

. . . .

. . . .

. . . .

. . . .

What frustrations do customers experience when receiving or picking upyour product or service ?

. . . .

. . . .

. . . .

. . . .

. . . .

What frustrations do customers experience when using your product or service?

. . . .

. . . .

. . . .

. . . .

. . . .

What frustrations do customers experience after they've bought your product or service?

. . . .

. . . .

. . . .

. . . .

. . . .

If you were a customer, why would you dislike buying from you?

. . . .

. . . .

. . . .

. . . .

. . . .

Describe the sort of customers who dislike buying from you ... and why?

. . . .

. . . .

. . . .

. . . .

. . . .

Unique Selling Proposition And Guarantee

Describe the sort of potential customers who love buying from you ... and why?

. . . .

. . . .

. . . .

. . . .

. . . .

If you could easily overcome any two of your customer's frustrations, what would they be and how would you overcome them?

1 . . . .

. . . .

. . . .

. . . .

. . . .

. . . .

2 . . . .

. . . .

. . . .

. . . .

. . . .

. . . .

What six things would relieve your customer's frustrations that you can guarantee and deliver 100% of the time right now?

1 . . . .

. . . .

. . . .

2 ....

....

....

3 ....

....

....

4 ....

....

....

5 ....

....

....

6 ....

....

....

What three additional things will you be able to fully guarantee within the next three months?

1 ....

....

....

2 ....

....

....

3 ....

....

....

Unique Selling Proposition And Guarantee

List three things you CAN'T confidently guarantee today, that you would love to be able to guarantee.

1 . . . .

2 . . . .

3 . . . .

What is the ONE thing that, if you could guarantee it, would make you the market leader? (For example, a news agency that guarantees to sell you a winning lottery ticket every time). Is there any way in the world, within the realms of human possibility, you could offer this, even if it backfired some of the time?

. . . .

. . . .

. . . .

. . . .

. . . .

. . . .

OK, from these questions you will have worked out a couple of things. Firstly, you would have probably noticed you can guarantee more than you thought, and secondly, that your customers experience frustrations throughout the entire buying process.

How can you match the two up - that is, how can you guarantee to remove the frustrations your customers have?

The best way is to completely forget about what you can do - let's think about what your customers want. Once you know this, let's work out how you can promise to give it to them.

OK, to begin with, let's work out what the biggest frustration customers have when dealing with you. For example, if it's builders dealing with sub-contractors, it's almost always people not turning up. If it's people getting their haircut, it's usually the hairdresser taking too much off and making them look silly. If it's a gym, it's often that they feel uncomfortable letting their blubber fly in front of a bunch of tanned, well-toned Greek gods and gym bunnies.

Think about what really bugs your customers. Get into their shoes and ask yourself this question: "If I could just find a [business type] that did [x], I'd deal with them every time and recommend them to all my friends."

OK, now fill in the blanks – what is that one thing? Got it? Now, how can you guarantee to do that for them? Don't immediately rule out the possibility - there are dentists out there that guarantee no pain, no waiting and no surprises. There are pest control companies that guarantee you won't SEE a bug for six months, there are hairdressers that guarantee to fit a hair extension free if they chop off too much, and there are video stores that will let you watch another video free if you don't like the one you've just hired. The impossible can be achieved.

Of course, that one thing may not be achievable – you have to ask yourself whether it's economically viable.

But if you can't deliver on the first one, let's move on to the next biggest frustration. Think about it – what else bugs your customers?

Now let's develop a guarantee based on that. Can't be done? Move onto the next one, but make sure you're giving each one a fair chance. If you're just avoiding a killer guarantee for fear of doing more work or having to re-arrange the business, you're cheating yourself.

Once you know what you want to guarantee, it's time to write it down. This will be promoted on all of your sales materials, in your ads and on your letterhead, so it pays to take time on it.

The basic format for a powerful guarantee is simple: 'If this doesn't happen, then we'll do that.' For example, 'If your friends don't start commenting on your immaculately clear skin within four weeks, you get every dollar back and a voucher for a free consultation with a dermatologist (value $80).' How much business is that guarantee going to get a beautician?

OK, let's write yours. Firstly, write the first part of your guarantee. This is where you promise something will happen. Make the actual promise as specific as you can. Put a time frame on it and make it really stand out. Explain what will happen and what the real benefits of buying the product or service are.

Secondly, write the 'this will happen' bit. Don't be afraid of offering their money back. Or you could offer to 'keep working with you until you get the results.'

Another option is 'we'll pay for you to see our most hated competitor' or 'we'll write you a cheque for the amount you invested, plus $1000 to go to your favourite charity.' Now that's powerful! Of course, it all depends on the industry your operating in.

Step 6: How (Do You Promote Your USP And Guarantee)?

It's important to get right behind your new USP & Guarantee – print them on your letterhead and business cards.

Here's an example:

Why you should buy from us? Because we have New Zealand's largest range of musical instruments and every member of staff is a professional musician with at least one top ten hit each. Our guarantee? If you don't believe you've bought the right instrument at the best possible price, you may return it within 14 days and we'll give you 20% off your next purchase.

Now if you have developed a USP & Guarantee as powerful as that, you'd be crazy if you didn't put it in every newspaper ad you ran and every letter you wrote. Why not write back to your past customers and let them know about your new policies. And whatever you do, don't forget your USP when it comes to writing your Yellow Pages ad. This is the place where people already know they want to buy from someone. They just need to know who. If you show them you are different and promise to take away one of their key frustrations, you'll find you get double the number of enquiries you did from your old ad.

Try it and find out.

The important thing to remember is this – now you've written your USP and Guarantee, it's important you promote it and tell people about it. It may solve every marketing problem you've ever had.

Step 7: What Else (Do You Need To Think About)?

Use this section as a final checklist. Once you're happy with your USP and Guarantee, run through and make sure you're ready to get started. Here are a few things you should consider:

Team Training: Does your team fully understand the ideas you've created? It's important that you communicate everything you've written and thought about. Your team needs to be informed of what's going on and how they should act now you are going to be positioning yourself differently.

Check that what you have created is truly unique: It's pretty common that your first effort is not unique - a competitor has probably already done it. Of course, if the idea has only been done overseas or interstate, then there shouldn't be a problem.

Unique Businesses And Powerful Guarantees

Here's a list of some ideas to get you thinking:

Hairdressing

Imagine a hairdresser that had cable TV and a full library of videos in the salon. While having your haircut, you could watch any TV channel, or any video you could think of. Expensive, but it would certainly bring people in. The hairdresser may also have a 'Talk-O-Meter', which ranges from 'Just the haircut' to 'I'm feeling chatty'. People either fill out a form before having their haircut or they could tell the hairdresser directly.

Restaurant

Instead of a range of meals at different prices, a restaurant could offer a specific number of meals (47, for example), all at one price ($8.95). You walk in, choose your meal and it arrives in 11 minutes or less. If it arrives late, or if it's not the tastiest meal you've had in ages, you get your next meal free. The marketing would probably be based on the 47 meals, all for $8.95, but it would also strongly feature the guarantee.

Florist

Imagine a florist that has a professional writer who helps you craft your message. You simply call up and say, 'I want to send roses to my wife. I crashed her car while driving my mistress around. Can you patch it up for me?" It'd be a tough job for the writer, but many people would love to send a personalised, well-written message of love to their spouse. The guarantee could be this: 'If our flowers don't put a smile on their face, we'll refund your money.' The florist could use flyers to promote this. Imagine a headline like: 'Problems with the wife? If our flowers don't put a smile on her face, you won't pay!'

Video Store

What about a video shop that also rents computer games, books, music and board games. It would then be more of an entertainment rental store.

Stationery

Imagine a stationery supplier who guaranteed the lowest prices and fastest delivery. The guarantee could read like this: 'If you can find anyone who beats our prices, we'll give you that item free. If you don't get your delivery within 40 minutes of your phone call, we'll buy you lunch anywhere in the CBD.' This could certainly be the basis of a strong marketing campaign. The stationery supplier could write letters to potential businesses with the headline: 'Tired of paying too much for stationery and waiting too long for it to be delivered?' Then the letter would outline the guarantee.

Convenience Store

Imagine a convenience store that offered a special incentive every time you spent more than $20. For example, automatic entry to a competition in which you get to roll three dice. If you roll three sixes, you win a $300 voucher to spend in the store. The competition would certainly be enough to build a marketing campaign on. Newspaper ads could say: 'Going grocery shopping?' then continues with an explanation of the competition. The hook could be: 'You won't pay more; parking's easy, you'll get through the checkout quicker and you have a chance of winning $300.'

Builder

What about a builder who guarantees to have your home finished two days before the deadline? If not, the builder will pay double your rent for every day the construction is overdue. Furthermore, the builder guarantees to have everything completely finished - there will be no loose ends, no unpainted sections, and everything will be exactly as you expect it to be.

Training Company

Imagine a corporate training company that guaranteed to get your team so fired up, you'd want to give them all a pay rise. It could read like this: 'Our training will transform your team. In fact, we bet you'll feel like giving them all a pay rise. If you don't, we'll cut the price in half and train your team again.' This could definitely be the beginning of a great marketing campaign. The headline could be: 'Imagine having a team of people so good you'll wish you could pay them all double - we guarantee to create this for you!'

Part 8

∎ Writing 'Killer' Headlines

If you're running a line or semi-display advertisement, you'll probably only be able to use one or two words in your headline. But choosing the right words is crucially important to your campaign. We'll look at those two forms of classified ads later. Firstly, lets look at effective headlines for full display classifieds.

Display Classifieds

The best headlines do three things – they identify the right target market, they provide benefits, and they generate enough interest to get them read.

Let's look at each one in more depth:

Identify The Right Target Market: You need to make sure your target market sees and reads your ad. Your headline needs to immediately speak to them. There's nothing wrong with starting your headline with 'MOTHERS' or even 'ATTENTION Ladies 37-40 with no children.'

Of course, there are other more subtle ways, such as 'Here's how to make your Ford go faster' or 'Help the kids succeed at school this year.'

Provide Benefits: You need to give your readers reasons to investigate further. Think about it. What is really going to make them want to read your ad? A headline such as 'MEN: How you can have twice as much sex as you're having now ... guaranteed' speaks for itself. What can you say about your product or service? What is the main benefit?

Once you've thought of that, try coming up with some more specific and interesting ways of phrasing it. For example, 'How you can make an extra $4500 this year and pay off those credit card debts' is more interesting than 'How you can make more money.'

Generate Interest: There's nothing more powerful than curiosity. Compare these two headlines: 'AMWAY: a new future for you' and 'How you can make $1100 extra per week by meeting three new people a month.' Both are for the same company, but one holds more interest value and is more likely to get you reading.

Try getting the main benefit across without telling the whole story. Try getting a bit of mystery in there. Of course, too much mystery can kill your ad. Who'd read an ad with a headline such as 'Pure grunt', 'Big cheese' or 'Stilted?' No-one, as so many advertisers have discovered.

Headline Starters

This is where you get to write potential headlines for your ad. You'll get a sharper focus of what you want to really say to potential customers, as well as learning what makes a headline work.

7 reasons

Firstly, write two headlines beginning with "7 reasons." Here are some examples:

> 7 reasons why YOU should call George's Widgets today.

> 7 reasons to get your Widget from George's.

Now it's your turn.

7 reasons . . . .

. . . .

. . . .

7 reasons . . . .

. . . .

. . . .

Here's why

Now, try two headlines beginning with "Here's why." Here are some examples:

> Here's why George's is offering YOU a FREE box of Widgets.

> Here's why YOU need to call George's Widgets now.

Now it's your turn.

Here's why . . . .

. . . .

. . . .

Here's why . . . .

. . . .

. . . .

Here's how

Next, try two headlines beginning with "Here's how." Here are some good examples:

> Here's how George's Widgets helps you live forever.
>
> Here's how to get the perfect Widget ... guaranteed.

Now it's your turn.

Here's how . . . .

. . . .

. . . .

Here's how . . . .

. . . .

. . . .

Announcing

Next, try two headlines beginning with "Announcing." Here are some examples:

> Announcing ... a Widget dealer that guarantees your delight.
>
> Announcing ... a guaranteed way to lose weight using Widgets.

Now it's your turn.

Announcing . . . .

. . . .

. . . .

Announcing . . . .

. . . .

. . . .

Writing 'Killer' Headlines

DON'T

Next, try two headlines beginning with "DON'T." Here are some great examples:

> DON'T take another breath until you read this.

> DON'T call anyone about Widgets until YOU speak to George's.

Now it's your turn.

DON'T . . . .

. . . .

. . . .

DON'T . . . .

. . . .

. . . .

New

Next, try two headlines beginning with "New." Here are some examples:

> New ... widgets that actually repair themselves.

> New cheaper way to buy widgets.

Now it's your turn.

New . . . .

. . . .

. . . .

New . . . .

. . . .

. . . .

Now

Lastly, try two headlines beginning with "Now." Here are some examples:

> Now available ... home hairdressing kits that your teenage daughter will like.

> Now in pre-production ... a movie based on the life of Elvis Presley.

Now it's your turn.

Now . . . .

. . . .

. . . .

Now . . . .

. . . .

. . . .

Line And Semi-Display Classifieds

Unlike display classifieds, line and semi-display classifieds are, as a rule, not big enough to allow headlines any larger than one or two words. However, these words must be chosen carefully if your advertisement is to bring the desired results.

One of the easiest ways to write an effective headline for a line ad or semi-display classified is to simply use the name of the product you're selling. For example, if you're a gardening store selling hoses, you'd simply use the word 'Hoses' as your headline. If you're a car yard advertising a number of vehicles, use the brand name of your best car, for example 'Ford Falcon EB'.

The reason why this approach works so well is simply because people who are looking in the classified section of their local paper will normally have a particular product in mind. So don't try to be too clever with your one or two word headlines as this is a surefire way to miss the sale.

To demonstrate this, let's look at our gardening store who are trying to sell hoses. If they were to run a headline that said: 'Outstanding Quality' their product would be listed under 'O' in the For Sale section. But people looking to buy a hose would look under 'H' for hoses.

Understand that you need to keep it simple if you want it to work.

There are two types of headlines which most newspapers offer, supposedly to assist you in making your product standout. These are normally referred to as Impact and Attention Grabbing headlines. Let's look at each one individually.

Impact: These are one or two word headlines are set in a larger point size than the rest of your ad. The increase in point size can be as much as double that of your body copy. These headlines are usually more expensive and are sold as being a great way to make your headline stand out. You're probably thinking this sounds like a good idea, particularly as we've already stated that the headline of a display ad should be much larger than the copy. But one of the downfalls of an impact headline is the fact they're almost always set in all capitals. SETTING YOUR HEADLINE IN ALL CAPITALS CAN MAKE IT VERY DIFFICULT TO READ. A more effective, and cheaper, way to make your headline, or first word, stand out is to use bold.

Attention Grabbers: These headlines are also more expensive, costing more again than an impact headline. Attention grabbers are large, and use unusual fonts and graphics to supposedly make them stand out. The problem is these fonts are usually San Serif fonts that are more difficult to read.

One of the other concerns when looking at these types of headlines is the fact that there can be dozens of them on the same page. This, of course, dramatically decreases their effectiveness. They are also, as a rule, made up of a standard set of words and pictures such as MOVING INTERSTATE or URGENT SALE, which means you can't have your product listed in the alphabetical order you want. In the end, anyone who's in the market for your type of product will look for it in the most obvious alphabetical place. In other words, if they're looking for a Ford Falcon EB, they'll probably go straight to the 'F' section of the car listings. The trick is to make sure your Falcon is there when they're looking.

Part 9

▋ Creating Powerful Offers

So you've written a great headline, an exciting first paragraph and sub-headlines that tell a story. But what are you going to do to get your target market to respond? Great copy alone won't work; you need a strong offer – an offer you would respond to yourself.

So what then is a great offer?

When thinking of what to offer your customers, ask yourself this: "If I read this ad, would the offer be good enough to make me respond?" If your answer is no, go back to the drawing board. Without a great offer, you cannot achieve great results.

Another thing to consider is the lifetime value of the people who respond to your ad. Taking a smaller profit in the short-term will generally work better in the long-run.

Here are some examples of powerful offers:

- Free haircut – for a hairdressing salon looking to increase its database.
- 2 Steak Dinners and 2 Glasses of Wine for $10 – restaurant recruiting members for its VIP Club.
- 1 New Release Video and a Large Pizza for $6 – video store promotion to recruit new members.

All these offers are worthwhile and are sure to get a great response. Weak offers will cause your ad to fail. Understand that your offer is the part of your ad that gets your customers to act now and to buy from you rather than your opposition.

Here are some examples of weak offers:

- 10% off – this is not a big enough discount to generate interest.
- Call now for your free colour brochure – so what?
- Buy 9 and get the 10th for ? price – no one would respond to this offer.

Types Of Offers

Here are some possibilities that would be worth considering:

The Added Value With Soft Dollar Cost

Soft Dollar Cost refers to products, services or added extras you can combine with your standard product to make it more attractive and to increase it's perceived value. These offers don't add much, if anything, to your costs. For this strategy to be effective, the added extra must have a high perceived value. In other words, your customers must see the added benefit as being great value.

The Package Offer

By packaging products and services together you create a more marketable combination. There is a higher 'perceived' value when products or services are packaged together. Your customers will want to buy more, simply because of the extra products they get when buying a product they already want. One of the best examples of a great package is computer equipment. Buy the hardware and receive the software for free. This style of offer is very attractive to potential customers.

Discounts vs. Bonus Offers

More often than not, discounting will cost you profits. A far better way of clearing stock and generating extra trade is to have a '2 for the price of 1' sale. Or, try a 'buy one of these and get one of these FREE.' Another way of saying this is 'every 10th purchase free,' or 'when you spend $100, we'll give you $20 off your next purchase.'

Valued At Offer

If you are including a free item in your ad, make sure you value it. For example, RING now for your FREE consultation, normally valued at $75. This positions your time, product, or service much more than a simple free give-away people won't value or appreciate.

Time Limited Offers

Place a time limit on your offer. Doing so will dramatically increase the response rate because it gives people a reason to respond right now. Place urgency in your offer. For a short time only ... Call before such and such ... Only while stocks last. These will all create a sense of urgency in your consumer's mind.

Guarantee Offers

Using a guarantee offer is a great way to boost the response to your ad. People will be far more willing to part with their money if you remove the risk from the buying decision. The better the guarantee you make, the higher your response rate will be.

FREE Offers

Giving away something absolutely free, with no catches whatsoever, is often a brilliant way to build a loyal customer base. Offer a "bribe" to get potential customers in through the door initially, then great service and products to encourage them to come back. This type of offer can reduce your "cost per lead" dramatically.

Part 10

∎ Break Even Analysis

Why It's Important

It's essential you work out your costs up front. Otherwise, you'll have no idea what you need to achieve in order for the campaign to be worthwhile.

You may find out after doing the analysis that the campaign has so little chance of success, you need to go back to the drawing board.

This analysis is for the whole campaign. After you've worked out your total fixed costs (for the campaign), you then work out your profit (your average dollar sale minus your variable costs), which gives you enough information to work out how many responses you need in order to break even. Here's an example of an analysis form:

Break Even Analysis

Lead Generation Campaign

Hard Costs

Advertising	$ . . . . . .
Envelopes	$ . . . . . .
Paper	$ . . . . . .
Printing	$ . . . . . .
Postage	$ . . . . . .
Other	$ . . . . . .
1. Total Fixed Costs	**$ . . . . . .**

2. Average $$$ Sale   **$ . . . . . .**

Variable Costs

Telephone	$ . . . . . .
Wages	$ . . . . . .
Electricity	$ . . . . . .
Rent	$ . . . . . .
Brochures	$ . . . . . .
Other Postage	$ . . . . . .
Other	$ . . . . . .

3. Total Variables $ . . . . .

Delivery Costs
    Cost Of Goods Sold $ . . . . . .
    Taxes $ . . . . . .
    Transportation $ . . . . . .
    Packaging $ . . . . . .
    Other $ . . . . . .
4. Total Delivery $ . . . . .

5. Net Profit [2/(3+4)] $ . . . . .

Conclusion

So there you have it – some really great strategies to help you generate more leads for your business.

Lead generation strategies serve a very important purpose in business – any business. They get customers or clients to consider doing business with you. You see, it's all very well having a great business and the best products or services around, but if you don't get people coming to you, you're wasting your time. Competition is fierce out there. There has never been more advertising clutter in the marketplace before. Customers, consumers or clients are literally being bombarded by advertising messages every minute of everyday. How will you ensure your message sticks and gets them to come to you, when there are all these other messages competing for their attention?

This book explains some of the more unusual, yet highly effective, means of generating leads, like cultivating Host Beneficiary strategies or developing a Unique Selling Proposition. Use these strategies to set yourself apart from your competition.

You may also find that, by concentrating on developing a set of lead generation strategies, you'll begin to see your business in a different light. You may discover things about it you never knew before. This alone could very well give you the advantage you're looking for.

Once you've worked your way through this book, you'll know how to write effective press, radio and Yellow Pages advertisements. You'll be amazed at how easy it is to write killer headlines and create powerful offers. You'll know what it takes to develop a strong Strategic Alliance and a host beneficiary relationship; you'll know the power of a Referral System. Your new Unique Selling Proposition and Guarantees that will have customers lining up to do business with you, will blow you away.

You'll also know how to analyse the costs involved and how to work out what your break-even point is.

But most importantly, you'll know how to quickly develop lead generation campaigns that will be the envy of your competitors.

So what are you waiting for? Get into *Action* now.

∎ Getting Into *Action* ...

So, when is the best time to start ?

NOW ... right now ... so let me give you a step-by-step method to get yourself onto the same success path many of my clients and the clients of my team at *Action* International have experienced.

Start testing and measuring now. Re-read Part 5 and work through the steps.

You'll want to ask each and every customer and prospect how they found out about you and your business. This will give you an idea of what's been working and what hasn't. You also want to concentrate on the five numbers of the business chassis. Remember ...

1. Number of Leads from each campaign.
2. Conversion Rate from each and every campaign.
3. Number of Transactions on average per year per customer.
4. Average Dollar Sale from each campaign.
5. Your Margins on each product or service.

The **Number of Leads** is easy, just take a measure for four weeks, average it out and multiply by 50 working weeks of the year. Of course you'd ask each lead where they came from so you've got enough information to make advertising decisions.

The **Conversion Rate** is a little trickier, not because it's hard to measure, but because we want to know a few more details. You want to know what level of conversion you have from each and every type of marketing strategy you use. Remember that some customers won't buy right away so keep accurate records on each and every lead.

To find the **Number of Transactions** you'll need to go through your records. Hopefully you can find the transaction history of at least 50 of your past customers and then average out their yearly purchases.

The **Average Dollar Sale** is as simple as it sounds. The total dollars sold divided by the number of sales. The best information you can collect is the average from each marketing campaign you run, so you know where the real profit is coming from.

And of course, your margins. An **Average Margin** is good to know and measure, but to know the margins on everything you sell is the most powerful knowledge you can collect.

Whilst you're collecting this information, re-read Parts 1 and 2 so you can be sure your mindset is ready for the growth of your business.

If you're having any trouble with your testing and measuring be sure to call your nearest **Action** *International* Business Coach. They'll be able to help you through and show you the specialised documents to use.

If, by chance, you're thinking of racing ahead before you test and measure, remember this. It's impossible to improve a score when you don't know what the score is.

So, you've got your starting point. You know exactly what's going on in your business right now. In fact, you know more about not only what's happening right now, but also the factors that are going to create what will happen tomorrow.

The next step in your business growth is simple.

Let's decide what you want out of the business. In other words, your goals. Here's the main points I want you to plan for.

Firstly, how many hours do you want to work each week? How much money do you want to take out of the business each month? And, most importantly, when do you want to finish the business?

By 'finish' the business, I mean, when will it be systematized enough so it will run without you. Remember this about business; a little bit of planning goes a long way, but to make a plan you have to have a destination.

Once again, if you're having difficulty talk to an **Action** *International* Business Coach. They'll know exactly how to help you find what it is you really want out of both your business and your life.

When you've got it down, then it's time to get your **Instant Marketing Plan** together ...

Here's how we'll do it ...

Go back to Part 4 of this book and fill in the various survey forms (if you haven't already done so) as well as the five **Killer Strategy Forms** relating to each of the five parts of the Business Chassis. That's right, the forms that get you to decide which of 5 Killer Strategies you will use for Number of Leads, Conversion Rate, Number of Transactions, Average Dollar Sale, and Margins. Together, these forms are your **Instant Marketing Plan.**

Now the real work begins.

Remember our goal is to get a 10% increase in each area over the next 12 months. Choose well, but I want to warn you of one thing. One thing I can literally guarantee.

8 out of 10 marketing campaigns you run WILL NOT WORK ...

That's why when you choose to run, say, an advertising campaign in your local newspaper, you've got to run at least ten different ads. When you select a direct mail campaign, you send out at least ten different letters to test, and so on.

Make sure you get at least five strategies under each heading and plan to run at least one, preferably two, at least each month for the next 12 months.

Don't work on just one of the five areas at a time; mix it up a little so you get the synergy of all five areas working together.

Now, this is the most important advice I can give you:

Learn how to make each and every strategy work. Don't just think you know what to do, go through my hints and tips, read more books, listen to as many tapes as you can, watch all the videos you can find, talk to the experts, and make sure you get the most advantage you can before you invest a whole lot of money.

The next 12 months are going to be a matter of doing the numbers, running the campaigns, testing headlines, testing offers, testing prices and, of course, measuring the results.

By the end of it you should have at least five new strategies in each of the five areas working together to produce a great result.

Once again I want to stress that this will work and this will make your business grow as long as YOU work it.

Is it simple? YES ...

Is it easy? NO ...

You'll have to work and work hard. If you can get the guidance of someone who's been there before you, then get it.

Whatever you do, start it now, start it today ... and most importantly, make the most of everyday. Your past does not equal your future; you decide your future right here and right now.

BE who you want to be, DO what you need to do, in order to HAVE what you want to have.

Positive thought without positive *Action* leaves you with positively *NOTHING*. I called my company *Action International*, not 'Theory International', or 'Yeah I read that book International' ... but, *Action International* ...

So, take the first step ... and get into *Action* ...

■ ABOUT THE AUTHOR -

Bradley J Sugars

Brad is an entrepreneur for many reasons. By the time he was just 28 years of age he was the International Chairman of a global franchise that he started with NO capital. He had his first business at age 15, made a lot of money by the age of 22, lost it all by 22 1/2, then paid back all his debts and financially retired at 26.

At the age of 15 he employed his friends as paper delivery boys and gleaned a few dollars for the papers they delivered. Since then his businesses have become a little more sophisticated, yet still based on the same principle of finding something people want to buy then selling it to them, making sure he charged well, and gave great service.

By the time he'd finished University, he had completed a Bachelor of Business-Accounting and worked in 27 different jobs; from gardener to pipe maker, pizza cook to radio announcer, and disc-jockey to accounts clerk. One thing he'd definitely learnt; very few people ever really gave anything their best.

As soon as he'd left Uni he got a job selling and invested every single dollar he earned into training himself. Courses on money, investing, sales, business, personal growth - you name it, he did a course in it. He knew that to achieve what he wanted out of life wasn't going to be about how hard he worked, but about how much he knew. By the time he was 21, he was running four retail stores and a photocopy management contract, earning a salary of $60,000 a year.

His mum almost had a heart attack when he told her that he had quit to go and work for himself. Being young and naive was probably a good thing. No capital, but a lot of smart ideas on how to create sales, how to market and how to lead a team of people. By the way, those retail stores increased profits by 39% in the nine months he was in charge.

He bought into a ladies fashion store, a 33% holding with no money down; just the ability to help them create sales. He increased sales by 93% over the first nine weeks and sold his interest back to the other partners just three months later. He did the same with a pizza manufacturing business; he took their product from just being sold into cafes and got it on the shelves of Woolworths, and almost every other small retailer in Queensland. He funded this growth with his earnings from the ladies wear store and was also doing some business consulting in his spare time.

It was this consulting that really led him to where he is today. One gentleman he offered his services to *(he used to give away two hours of his time for free, just so people could understand what he could do for them)* ran an international training company.

This gentleman, Robert Kiyosaki, a best selling author, asked him to come and train his seminar promoters in the art of marketing. Little did he know then what was in store for him.

Training 30 seminar promoters in Hawaii meant that he was bound to go into the presenting business. Seminars in Hong Kong, New Zealand and in Melbourne meant the sale of the pizza business to create an international operation training and consulting to business owners and managers. Robert asked him to train at his Business School for Entrepreneurs in Hawaii later that year. That was July 1994, and 350 business owners from around the world, 11 trainers (mostly in their 40's and 50's) were there to learn from Brad. He found a business partner who could take care of the operations back home while he got out and presented seminars, did consulting and basically generated the cashflow. And that he certainly did with hundreds of seminars, as many plane flights all over Australia, New Zealand, Asia and into the United States resulting.

He arrived home in January 1995 to find not only was he was not only tired, sick of travel, and missing regular business, but he was also broke. Major business lesson number one; partnerships don't always work. What to him was VERY serious debt caused him to move back into his parents house, get a phone line connected, put a desk next to his bed and start all over again.

He almost went and got a job. And, as he'd just spent the last 11 months teaching everyone else how to make money (and getting great results for them), he spent three full days just sitting quietly wondering why he couldn't seem to do the same for himself. At the time he thought that life could never get any worse.

He sent a letter to every one of his past clients, seminar attendees and everyone else he knew, offering his consulting services again. And, after a few solid days on the phone, he was back in business. He sat down and wrote out the Vision, Mission and Culture Statement of the new company he was going to create. He decided to stay in the business of training business owners, but this time he'd be sure to do it well.

In March of that year his best friend from University began working with him. They worked from Brad's parents' 'granny flat'. Brad recorded sets of tapes while doing the seminars, kept selling and consulting during the day, and continued selling the tapes. They stayed back until about 10 or 11 each night planning and systemising.

It wasn't long before he'd paid back everything, saved a few dollars, and had a plan in place to create an amazing worldwide organisation. To cut a long story short, within three years and after many trials and tribulations, he managed to create a company called *Action International*. Employing 24 people in Australia, they took care of the business in Australia and New Zealand. A joint venture deal (worth several millions of dollars) was then signed to open an office in Singapore to service

South East Asia and in 1998 he took the big decision to go global through franchising. 188,000 people had attended *Action* seminars by then, 14,300 had been through their intensive workshops, and 397 had benefited from *Action* consulting services.

Brad is available for a limited number of speaking engagements each year. If you are interested in booking Brad as a keynote speaker for your next annual conference or business event, call *Action* International on +61 (7) 3368 2525. It's literally guaranteed that your attendees will say he's "the best speaker we've ever had," time and time again.

▮ RECOMMENDED READING LIST

ACTION INTERNATIONAL BOOK LIST

" The only difference between YOU now and YOU in 5 years time will be the people you meet and the books you read ..." Charlie 'tremendous' Jones

"And, the only difference between YOUR income now and YOUR income in 5 years time will be the people you meet, the books you read, the tapes you listen to, and then how YOU apply it all ..." Brad Sugars

- The E-Myth Revisited by Michael E. Gerber
- My Life in Advertising & Scientific Advertising by Claude Hopkins
- Tested Advertising Methods by John Caples
- Building the Happiness Centered Business by Dr. Paddi Lund
- Write Language by Paul Dunn & Alan Pease
- 7 Habits of Highly Effective People by Steven Covey
- First Things First by Steven Covey
- Awaken the Giant Within by Anthony Robbins
- Unlimited Power by Anthony Robbins
- 22 Immutable Laws of Marketing by Al Reis & Jack Trout
- 21 Ways to Build a Referral Based Business by Brad Sugars
- 21 Ways to Increase Your Advertising Response by Mark Tier
- The One Minute Salesperson by Spencer Johnson & Larry Wilson
- The One Minute Manager by Spencer Johnson & Kenneth Blanchard
- The Great Sales Book by Jack Collis
- Way of the Peaceful Warrior by Dan Millman
- How to Build a Championship Team - 6 Audio tapes by Blair Singer
- Brad Sugars "Introduction to Sales & Marketing" 3 hour Video
- Leverage - Board Game by Brad Sugars

*To order products from the recommended reading list call *Action International* **on +61 (7) 3368 2525**

■ Get Stacks of CASH and Heaps of CUSTOMERS ...

... get your ads designed by our Champion Creative Team ...

As you've just seen there's a lot to remember when it comes to writing effective ads. Well imagine having a team of marketing professionals design your ads for you ...

You will have some of the best in the country writing and designing your ads for you. Professionals who have created thousands of profitable advertisements and marketing campaigns.

Imagine having a Yellow Pages ad that has your phone ringing off the hook, or a Print Ad that has customers flocking through your door. Maybe you'd like an irresistible Sales Script that make prospects feel compelled to buy, or a Referral Strategy that generates hundreds of qualified, cost effective new leads. Our team of copywriters and graphic artists can give you all this and more ...

You can have our Champion Creative Team design a Web-site that will have the orders flooding in, or a Direct Mail campaign that turns your mail box into an amazing profit generating centre. If you're looking to change your image, imagine having our Champion Creative Team design your new Corporate Image or Logo. Best of all we give you a dozen variations on your ads for you to test and measure, so you can be sure to find one that gets amazing results.

Our team is not focussed on being 'clever' or winning awards. For years they've honed their skills in creating campaigns with one goal in mind ... Making Our Clients MONEY.

Being in business is not about doing it all yourself, it's about Leverage. It's about getting outside professionals doing the work for you, so your time is free to focus on growing your business and reaping the rewards. So why spend hours trying to design ads yourself, when you can have our creative team put together a sales and profit focused campaign that will have the money rolling in, in no time.

Call our team TODAY on 1800 670 335, and have us get started on your MONEY MAKING Campaign.

NEW RELEASE

AUD $34.95
(Incl. GST)

Billionaire In Training

90% of the stuff in this book is missing from most of the wealth creation manuals which are available on the market today ...

Designed to save aspiring Entrepreneurs a lot of mistakes, Billionaire In Training provides an essential framework for creating business success including strategies for increasing profit; a how-to guide for buying, selling and keeping businesses, how to keep yourself on track and moving toward your goals, the 5 Levels of an Entrepreneur and how to advance yourself to the upper levels.

NEW RELEASE

AUD $34.95
(Incl. GST)

Successful Franchising

The simple ice cream and milk shake may have a lot to answer for. You see, not only did they evolve into one of the most quintessential of all American icons; they've also got a lot to do with the birth of a whole new way of doing business. You see, they were at the centre of the evolution of a new business system that became known as franchising.

This book aims at putting franchising as a business method into perspective. It contains all the information you might need if you are buying a franchise, selling one or taking your existing business to the next level and franchising it.

NEW RELEASE

AUD $29.95
(Incl. GST)

Real Money Real Estate

Want to know how to buy property without outlaying any of your own cash? Can't be done? Not possible? Out of the question in a BOOM market?

If this is what you believe, then you're in for a HUGE surprise!

There are ways to buy property without using any cash. These strategies have generated us massive riches. In this book we will show you how to use them step-by-step. This book shows you the secrets to becoming financially free FAST. It shows you how we retired young and rich.

Leverage:
The Game of Business

The rewards start flowing the moment you start playing ...

Leverage is a educational breakthrough that'll have you quickly racking up the profits.

AUD $295.00
(Incl. GST)

The principles you take from playing this game will set you up for a lifetime of business success. It'll alter your perception and open your mind to what's truly possible. Sit back and watch your profits soar.

$ales Rich Video/DVD Series

Now you can learn the sales secrets that allowed Brad Sugars to financially retire at the age of 26. And, unlike most gurus, he started with NOTHING.

Take advantage of the only multi-millionaire who will teach you exactly how he did it. In this six-video set, Brad gives you more than just theory; he gives you practical step-by-step instructions to take you from being just an average sales person to becoming a SALES SUPERSTAR. And all for just $495.

AUD $495.00
(Incl. GST)

Millionaire In Training Video

Whether you've read the book or not, you've just got to view this video. Watch Brad Sugars in action as he fires up his audience, imparting powerful business secrets in an easy-to-understand fashion.

Not only will you find this best-selling video great value at $59, you'll find it very informative and highly entertaining. It's no wonder he's widely regarded as one of the world's leading business speakers.

AUD $59.00
(Incl. GST)

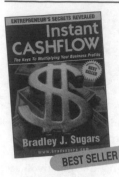

BEST SELLER

AUD $29.95
(Incl. GST)

Instant Cashflow
(Revised Edition)

Now you can learn Brad's most amazingly powerful and user-friendly sales and marketing tips all in one book.

This book will complement everything you will learn at Brad's Seminar. You will read this book once, then refer to it again and again!

There are so many simple, easy and ready-to-use tips on how to boost your bottom line that you'll have to refer it to your family and friends as well.

NEW RELEASE

AUD $29.95
(Incl. GST)

Instant Leads

One of the fundamental problems most businesses face is the generation of new leads. Without a constant supply of leads, they're faced with a never-ending battle to generate sufficient cashflow for the business to survive from one month to the next.

This book is designed to give you the inside track on everything you need to know about how to generate more leads for your business. It aims at providing you with an INSTANT guide on how to produce the various lead generation tools just like the professionals.

NEW RELEASE

AUD $29.95
(Incl. GST)

Instant Sales

By reading this book, you'll discover the secrets of selling. You'll also discover that the sales process actually starts well before you get to the stage of meeting your prospect face-to-face. You may even be surprised to discover this process actually starts with YOU.

In this book, Brad Sugars explains how to maximise your Conversion Rate, or to put it another way, how to make sure your prospects actually buy from you. He also explains some not-so-well-known techniques that are aimed at smoothing your path through the sales process.

Instant Promotions

Brad Sugars knows a thing or two about promoting a business. Learn his secrets and follow his easy-to-understand and simple-to-implement steps to promotional success that will put your business on the map.

This book is designed to give you the inside track on everything you need to know about promoting your business. It aims to provide you with an INSTANT guide on how to produce the various promotional items just like the professionals. Once you've read the book, you'll know precisely what it takes to successfully promote your business.

Instant Repeat Business

Hanging on to an existing customer is far easier, and much cheaper, than looking for new ones. Yet few business people realise this.

This book is all about looking after repeat business. It's all about ensuring your existing client-base remains happy, loyal and content. It's all about ensuring you look after that 20% of your customer-base that accounts for 80% of your turnover. It's all about turning your existing customers into your most prized asset – Raving Fans.

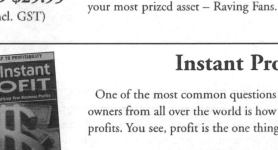

Instant Profit

One of the most common questions I get asked by business owners from all over the world is how they can improve their profits. You see, profit is the one thing they all want more of.

And that's understandable, because PROFIT is the very thing they are all in business for.

This book will teach you all you need to know about how to increase the profit your business makes. Think of it as a road map to profitability. Follow the general gist of the book or implement the strategies as they are; the choice is yours.

NEW RELEASE

AUD $29.95
(Incl. GST)

Instant Team Building

Do you know that a business is a reflection of its owner? Do you know that, as a business owner, you only get the people you deserve?

This book is designed to give you the inside track on everything you need to know about how to transform your staff into a dream team and how to become a great leader. It aims at providing you with an INSTANT easy-to-follow guide on how to go about making sure the people you select are just perfect for your business.

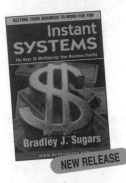

NEW RELEASE

AUD $29.95
(Incl. GST)

Instant Systems

This book is all about getting your business to work for you, rather than the other way round. It shows you all you need to know about how to work ON your business instead of IN it.

This book is your step-by-step guide to systems and how to introduce them into your business. It will transform your business, freeing you up so you can devote time to other things like being with your family, starting another business or really looking for investment bargains in the real estate market.

NEW RELEASE

AUD $29.95
(Incl. GST)

Instant Referrals

One of the most fundamental functions of any business is to ensure it has a constant supply of new leads to attempt to do business with. And it really doesn't matter what type of business you run, you simply need someone to do business with otherwise you can't claim to be in business.

This book is all about building a referral-based business. It will tell you everything you need to know about how to go about building a business that will build itself. It will tell you why this is the best type of business you could possibly want and how you can go about delivering the WOW factor to your customers time and time again.

Instant Advertising

149 Hints, Tips and Strategies on writing Ads that Sell

Armed with all of Brad's super powerful advertising hints and tips, you'll be ready to write super profitable ads in no time at all ...

With Instant Advertising, you'll quickly learn how to create profitable strategies and then how to create the ads that make the strategies work ... You'd be mad to pass up the opportunity to get this book.

AUD $29.95
(Incl. GST)

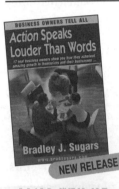

Action Speaks Louder Than Words

This book is about ordinary business people achieving astonishing results through business coaching. It chronicles the experiences of 17 businesses and outlines how they achieved phenomenal growth. You'll discover that the only real way to achieving amazing results for your business lies through business coaching. And you'll see it doesn't matter what type of business you run, how old or new your business is, how small or big, or even in what economy you're operating in, coaching can produce unimaginable results.

AUD $29.95
(Incl. GST)

Order all your Brad Sugars' products online ...

Getting hold of Brad Sugars' books and other products is now easier than ever before. Simply log on to bradsugars.com and buy online – it's as simple as that. Bookmark this site and keep up to date with the latest information from one of the world's leading business experts.

www.bradsugars.com

▌Double or Triple Your Profits Over the Next 12 Months ...

... and actually work less than half the hours you're currently working ...

This is the most important business workshop you'll ever attend ...

Take your business, whether it's running profitably, making a loss, or even just the seed of an idea and invest 5 days learning and applying strategies that will make you a marketing master. You'll leave the program with a bunch of strategies and ideas that will have your business flying. PLUS, you'll leave with a heap of ads and letters ready to generate real cash for you the moment you get back to your business.

Over the 5 days of Brad Sugars' MARKETING OVERHAUL WORKSHOP you'll discover the most powerful formula for creating cashflow in the world of business. You'll cover more than 70 different ways to generate leads. We will show you dozens of ways to increase the response to your advertising, and actually manage to spend less than you're currently spending.

You'll discover how to increase your conversion rate. It's great to get more enquiries, but it's pointless if you don't make sales. With just a couple of simple techniques you'll be able to sell to more people, without ever needing to offer a discount, or cut into your margins.

You'll probably also like to hear the 5 easiest ways to get your customers coming back more often. I'll take a moment to show you why this one simple idea can be the difference between a business that makes money, and one that goes to the wall. Imagine being able to get each customer spending more when they come into your business. You'll get 53 different strategies, any number of which could increase your cash flow overnight.

We'll also have a talk to you about your margins. It's one thing to have a good turnover, but at the end of the day, we're in business to make money. I'll let you in on 67 strategies that we've used in the past to help business owners make more out of each sale. PLUS you'll learn how to leverage yourself out of your business so you can start working 'ON' your business rather than 'IN' it. You'll also learn how to attract, motivate and keep top class employees.

The MARKETING OVERHAUL WORKSHOP will do more than simply teach you a few marketing strategies. It will give you the mindset of success, and the tools to achieve your business goals. If you want to get ahead of the pack you MUST attend this workshop.

Places in this course are strictly limited. To reserve your place call *Action International* TODAY. *Action International* Australia and New Zealand +61 (0)7 3368 2525

Free call within Australia 1800 670 335
Free call within New Zealand 0800 440 335
United States of America (888) 483 2828

I Entrepreneurs Training, Where You Discover How to Make Your Wildest Dreams a Reality ...

And, here's why we won't let most people attend this training program...

Never before has there been a workshop like this. Presented by entrepreneur and marketing guru Brad Sugars, this workshop will teach you everything you'll ever need to know about personal wealth, lifestyle and business success. It will change your life in the most positive way imaginable.

The Entrepreneurs Training is not open to everyone. In fact, it's open only to those who share a common goal - the desire to succeed.

Whether you're looking to make the most of your personal wealth, or increase the cashflow of your business, this 5 day, live-in workshop, will provide you with memorable gifts that will remain with you for the rest of your life.

This workshop is strictly invitation only. You'll need more than just money and time to attend this course. You'll need to embrace the workshop's motto - 'Whatever it takes'. 100% full on from the word go, you'll work hard, play hard and learn the level of performance you'll need to work at to create the entrepreneurial success you're after ...

If you could imagine what it would be like to achieve everything you've ever dreamt of, and have 100% trust in yourself, you'll understand why the *Action* Entrepreneurs Training is strictly Employees Not Allowed. You can never live in a state of fear, or work from an unleveraged place again after you've lived through these 5 days ...

You don't make a fortune running businesses, you make a fortune selling them. Discover how to take every business you have and turn it into capital growth. Unlike property, shares or any other form of investment, you can massively increase the value of your investment in a very short space of time, reaping the rewards both along the way and when you sell.

This workshop will do more than simply teach you how to make money. It's about discovering who you are, and who you want to be. You're guaranteed to get more out of The Entrepreneurs Workshop than any other workshop you've been to in the past.

This workshop is an absolute must. Call *Action International* TODAY to reserve your place. *Action International* Australia & New Zealand +61 (0)7 3368 2525

Free call within Australia 1800 670 335
Free call within New Zealand 0800 440 335
Free call within United States of America (888) 483 2828

▮ *Action* Contact Details ...

Action International Asia Pacific

Ground Floor, ***Action*** House, 2 Mayneview Street, Milton QLD 4064

Ph: +61 (0) 7 3368 2525

Fax: +61 (0) 7 3368 2535

Free Call: 1800 670 335

Action International UK & Ireland

3-5 Richmond Hill, Richmond, Surrey TW10 6RE

Ph: +44 (0) 208 948 5151

Fax: +44 (0) 208 948 4111

Action International North America

5670 Wynn Road Suite A & C, Las Vegas, Nevada 89118

Ph: +1 (702) 795 3188

Fax: +1 (702) 795 3183

Free Call: (888) 483 2828

Action Offices around the globe:

Australia I Canada I China I England I Hong Kong I India I Indonesia
Ireland I Malaysia I Mexico I New Zealand I Phillipines I Scotland I Singapore
USA I Wales

■ ATTENTION BUSINESS OWNERS ...
Increase your business profits

Here's how you can have one of Brad's *Action* Business Coaches guide you to success...

Like every successful sporting icon or team, a business needs a coach to help it achieve it full potential. In order to guarantee your business success you can have one of Brad's teams as your business coach. You will learn about how you can get amazing business results with the help of the team at *Action International*.

The business coaches are ready to take you and your business on a journey that will reward you for the rest of your life. You see, we believe *Action* speaks louder than words.

Complete & post this card to discover how the team at *Action* can help you increase your income today...

Action International ... **Business Trainers and Consultants ...**

The World's Number 1 Business Coaching Team

Name . . . .

Position . . . .

Company . . . .

Address . . . .

. . . .

Phone . . . .

Fax . . . .

E-mail . . . .

Referred by . . . .